THE POWER OF DICTATION

Pro tips for authors:

Make Dragon® software work for you

MARY CRAWFORD

Diversity Ink Press
Mary Crawford
www.MaryCrawfordAuthor.com

Identifiers

ISBN — 978-1-945637-18-6
ASIN — B07HDT855X

Book Design — Deena Rae Schoenfeldt — E-BookBuilders

Published October, 10, 2018, by Diversity Ink Press & Mary Crawford
Author may be reached at MaryCrawfordAuthor.com

Printed in The United States of America

Dedication

This book is dedicated to

Linda James and Larry Allen

These two individuals changed my world in ways they never could have imagined.

As my vocational rehabilitation counselor, Linda James, you believed I could do anything and helped me believe the same.

Larry Allen of Softnet, one of the early suppliers of voice recognition software and equipment who helped make it possible for me to reach all of my dreams.

I can never thank the two of you enough.

Table of Contents

Urgent Advisory from the Author

Dear Readers:

Quite literally on the eve of the publication of this book, Nuance® dropped Dragon® Professional Individual for Mac from its product lineup. They will continue to provide support for ninety days after October 22, 2018. After that, the future of Dragon for Mac remains uncertain. I have no word about whether a replacement product is being developed.

As I've stated in this book, I believe Dragon® Professional Individual 6.0.8 for Mac is a powerfully accurate product which can be a useful tool for authors. I use it every single day, and I am currently using it with Apple's new operating system, Mojave. I am not certain what spurred this development, but whatever the cause, I'm sad to see it. At the time of publication, Dragon® Professional Individual 6.0.8 for Mac is still available from other retailers such as Amazon and Best Buy.

To keep you informed with the latest breaking news, I've created a dedicated page on my website to The Power of Dictation. As soon as I have more information, I will share it with you at:

MaryCrawfordAuthor.com/The_Power_of_Dictation_News

Other Books by Mary Crawford

Hidden Beauty Series

Until the Stars Fall from the Sky
So the Heart Can Dance
Joy and Tiers
Love Naturally
Love Seasoned
Love Claimed
If You Knew Me (and other silent musings) (novella)
Jude's Song
The Price of Freedom (novella)
Paths Not Taken
Dreams Change (novella)
Heart Wish (100% charity release)
Tempting Fate
The Letter

Hidden Hearts Series:

Identity of the Heart
Sheltered Hearts
Hearts of Jade

Port in the Storm (novella)
Love is More Than Skin Deep
Tough
Rectify
Pieces (a crossover novel)
Hearts Set Free
Freedom (a crossover novel)
Love and Injustice

OTHER WORKS:

The Power of Dictation
Vision of the Heart
#AmWriting: A Collection of Letters to Benefit The Wayne Foundation

THE **POWER** OF **DICTATION**

Chapter 1

Introduction: What's the Big Deal?

What's So Powerful About Dictation?

If you've been hanging around in authors' circles recently, you have probably heard about voice recognition software. Maybe you know someone who uses it, or perhaps you use it yourself. Chances are you've heard things on both extremes. Either you've heard it is the miracle cure to all of your productivity problems or it's a nightmare to use and not worth trying.

Although I have heard wild tales of authors being able to write twenty-five thousand words an hour, that certainly is not my experience — even under the best of circumstances. I have severe cerebral palsy and I have been using voice recognition software since 1986. To be fair, my speed is likely impacted by the nature of my disability. I've never been known as a speed demon when it comes to dictation. I am, however, persistent. I know several authors who routinely dictate three to four thousand words an hour. There are many who can dictate faster. Dictation is certainly a boon to their productivity.

You may also hear the stories of how difficult it is to use voice recognition software. Some people find it challenging to use, especially in an environment where they need to be creative. The creative thought process seems to make using voice recognition software just a little more difficult.

Voice recognition software is not for everyone. There are some challenges which make it a tool of diminishing returns. Many of the obstacles can be overcome or worked around. I will discuss those later. I guess the message I want you to take from this book is that — just like other tools such as an ergonomic chair, keyboard, or mouse — voice recognition software is merely a tool you can use to better utilize your computer. Not every tool will work for every person. It doesn't mean you somehow failed, it just means the product didn't meet your expectations. I feel that way every time I try to use a traditional mouse. I much prefer a trackpad. It's not a matter of which input device is better than the other. What matters is that it works for you.

If you are approaching voice recognition software as a skeptic, I don't blame you — it's a little mystical and seems a bit too good to be true. Other authors use voice recognition software quite differently. I have used it more than half my life and use it for nearly every task I do on the computer. Every year, I dictate about a million words and publish around seven hundred thousand of them using Dragon® Dictate. On the other hand, most authors I know dictate part-time using Dragon® NaturallySpeaking. There is no right or wrong way to incorporate voice recognition software into your life.

My purpose in writing this book is to introduce voice recognition software as another tool in your toolbox as an author. I want to make it less intimidating, more accessible and give you some helpful, concrete tips to help you use voice recognition software more efficiently to speed up your writing process.

You may have already tried voice recognition software and found it difficult to use, or you may have heard horror stories from other authors. I get it. New software is hard to use, and it's hard to learn a new system.

If you'll indulge me for a moment, I'd like to take you on a trip down memory lane. For some of us, this trip takes a little longer than others. I'd like you to remember back to the first time you took a keyboarding class. Things that seem second nature now were not intuitive then. The keyboard felt foreign and your progress was slow and tedious. You made lots of mistakes. It was hard to remember what to do and what order in which you had to do things. Which command meant save? Where was the letter E again? How did I stop that stupid caps lock key from engaging? Did I have the printer set up correctly? Why was it spitting paper at me? (Maybe that was only me and my deranged printer...)

For those of us who learned on typewriters, there were even more moving parts. There were carriage returns, changing the ribbon, self-correcting ribbons and the proper use of whiteout.

Every new technology you learn is daunting in the beginning. It's often slow and tedious. We tend to forget those challenges as we master each new technology and move onto the next. This is especially true for skills we learned when we are young.

If you're feeling discouraged in the beginning, give yourself some grace. There's a learning curve when you learn new things. Becoming truly comfortable with voice-recognition technology may take some time. It doesn't come naturally to everyone. You will get better with practice. For most people, unless you have an injury or a disability which requires you to use voice recognition software, your adoption of this technology doesn't have to be an all-or-nothing proposition. You can ease your way into adopting a new way of doing things.

Who is Mary Crawford?

If you're anything like I am, when you pick up a book like this, the first thing you wonder is what makes the author qualified to tell you anything about the subject at hand. I'm happy to tell you I am a prolific author who uses Dragon® Dictate every day. In fact, I've used voice recognition software for thirty years.

As I mentioned, I was an early adopter of voice recognition software because I have severe cerebral palsy and it is difficult for me to type. Back in those days Dragon® NaturallySpeaking was considered a rehab tool and was very expensive. A setup cost nearly $3,000. Fortunately, I had a counselor through the Vocational Rehabilitation Division who understood that Dragon® would be critical to my success as a college student. I flirted a bit with a competing product back in the early days called Kurzweil, but the program didn't stick around long. I quickly returned to Dragon® NaturallySpeaking.

As a person with a severe motor impairment, I not only dictated my papers, I used the legal version of Dragon® NaturallySpeaking to take my essay exams during law school and to take the bar exam. When I first went to law school, I made a stupid, shortsighted decision. I didn't want to be treated any differently than my classmates, despite my obvious limitations. For my first set of exams, I didn't choose to use my voice recognition software. It was the dumbest decision I made during my law school career. It took me the rest of the time I was in law school to recover from the grades I earned that semester. My cerebral palsy prevented me from typing like the other students. I had the knowledge in my head; I was just unable to get it out on paper without assistive technology. Needless to say, I quickly reversed my decision and asked for the appropriate accommodations and received them.

I worked a variety of jobs as a civil rights attorney. I was the legal advisor for civil rights for the Forest Service, the Director of Disability Services for a small university and legal counsel for a center serving victims of domestic violence. I also served in many volunteer capacities with the Oregon State Bar.

I had to reinvent myself again when health problems disrupted my career as an attorney. In June of 2014, I published my first book, a contemporary romance novel. Four years later, I have now written or contributed to thirty.

When I was growing up struggling to hold a pencil or cursing my way through keyboarding class (and boy did I curse under my breath), I never in a million years thought I would become an author to write one book, let alone thirty. Voice recognition software opened that world to me.

Voice recognition changed my life. I hope it can help you in similar ways. Let's get started with some basic concepts. First, I'll talk about what voice recognition software is and if it might be right for you.

Throughout this book you may notice I've highlighted different types of tips. I have divided them into three different types. If the tips relate directly to dictation, you will see a microphone graphic like this:

If the tip is more general and designed to help you become a power user of voice recognition software, it will look like this:

Sometimes, I will caution you against a potential pitfall or problem. In those cases, I will flag the tip with this graphic:

Chapter 2

What Is Voice Recognition Software and Is It for You?

What Is Dictation?

When I tell people I use voice recognition software, many people aren't familiar with the concept or they are intimidated by it. I often get asked, "What is that exactly?"

In its simplest terms, it's just another way to input data into the computer. It's an alternative to your keyboard. Not that I'm suggesting you throw out your keyboard or anything — that would just be awkward. Although, you can use Dragon® NaturallySpeaking completely hands-free if you need to. It takes time and dedication to use it in this mode.

You probably already use voice recognition software in other contexts without even thinking about it. When you use the voice search feature on your phone, it is a form of voice recognition software. When your credit card company asks you to answer yes or no or enter your ZIP Code using your voice, it utilizes the same technology. Those of you who find the prospect of using entirely new technology paralyzing can relax. It's not new technology. You've likely been using it in various forms for years.

Nuance®, the company who distributes Dragon® Dictate and Dragon® NaturallySpeaking, developed the software behind Siri. So, if you use Siri to find the latest weather forecast or your favorite takeout place, you are already familiar with the basics of voice recognition software.

If you are new to dictation, I strongly encourage you to use Siri, the voice features of Google search and the dictation features in your operating system on your iPhone or Android phone to get used to the idea of dictating. The more often you speak your ideas out loud, the easier it will become. Soon, dictating will become like second nature.

Will Dictating Make Me Write Faster?

A common question I receive when people find out I dictate my work often sounds a bit like this, "That's cool, Mary, but I type X amount of words per minute, do you really think I can dictate faster than that?"

My honest answer is I don't know. Like typing, dictation is a very individual thing. There are many reasons you shouldn't base your probability of success on me. First, I've been using voice recognition software for thirty years; it's second nature for me. If you don't believe me, you should hear one of my voicemails. It sounds something like this, "Hi, comma this is Mary period. I'm sorry I missed you today period. I'll try to call tomorrow period." You probably think I'm joking, but sadly I'm not. My husband and my children have received many strange messages like this. Once you get in the habit, it's hard to change your ways.

 There are many opportunities to dictate in everyday life. Try to take advantage of these. It will help you get over your fear of speaking your thoughts out loud.

Another reason my speed — or lack thereof — isn't an accurate indicator of how well you will do is because I've had an intractable migraine for the last sixteen years. My cerebral palsy is affected by how well I feel. If I am fatigued or in pain, my speech is even more slurred. As you might guess, Dragon® doesn't respond favorably to slurry speech. Some days, it's a fight to get any words down. Even so, using voice recognition is far faster for me than typing. My cerebral palsy adversely affects my hands and my fine motor control. I am an abysmal typist.

Other people struggle much less than I do and can achieve very impressive speeds. I have heard anecdotal stories of authors achieving astronomical numbers. However, most authors I know who do quite well with voice recognition software and can produce around four to five thousand words in an hour. That's still an impressive amount of words.

Let's be real. It is very unlikely you'll achieve those numbers on the first day you install any voice recognition product on your computer. It takes practice to get the rhythm down and to rewire your brain to speak your story instead of type it.

I'm often asked if it's worth it to use voice recognition software if you're a reasonably fast typist. My answer to that question is most likely yes.

Repetitive stress injuries are no joke. Typing is hard on your wrists, elbows, shoulders, and neck. If you can relieve the strain on your body, even for just a few hours a day, it's a win.

 Even using voice recognition software part-time will relieve the wear and tear on your body and reduce your risk for repetitive stress injuries.

One of the reasons I decided to cover such a broad spectrum of products in a single book is because there are so many ways to use voice activation software. I use it full-time and barely type at all. Although I began my voice recognition journey with Dragon® NaturallySpeaking, these days I primarily use Dragon® Dictate on a Mac and very rarely transcribe. On the other hand, most of my author friends use Dragon® NaturallySpeaking on Windows and dictate part-time. Several of them are avid fans of transcription. There is no one correct way to use voice recognition software, it is merely a tool to make writing easier for you.

Does It Always Work?

I'm going to say something here you might not expect me to say. After all, this is a book all about the power of dictation and how it can change your life as an author. But, if you know me in person or you've come to know me over the Internet, you know I'm nothing but brutally honest. The truth is, voice recognition software is not a one-size-fits-all-fix-everything Band-Aid for every person who tries to use it. For some people, it's just not the right tool.

How can you tell if it may not be the right tool for you *before* you invest the money?

If you have a speech impediment which makes it difficult for you to articulate words, you may find voice recognition software frustrating to use. Having said that, over the past five years or so, the technology has become much more forgiving. If you want to try it, you should purchase your voice recognition software directly from Nuance®. They allow returns within the first thirty days.

The same is true for individuals with strong accents. This is a situation in which Dragon® NaturallySpeaking has more options than Dragon® Dictate. Dragon® NaturallySpeaking allows you to more finely tune your profile to your accent. It also allows you to set up a profile as a teen. If you are a woman with a high or soft voice, sometimes using a teen profile is a better option.

There's one more factor many people tend to overlook when they try to figure out whether voice recognition will work for them. Environment plays a key role in whether your experience with dictation will be successful. No voice recognition software app can think like a human brain. It cannot filter out extraneous noise. It is critical that the environment in which you dictate be relatively quiet. Once again, the software has made a great deal of progress in recent years, filtering out random noises like the television or voices in the next room. Still, your dictation will be more accurate and faster in a quiet environment.

If you have no control over your environment, you may find using voice recognition software challenging. Some folks get around this by using the transcription feature and taking their dictation mobile. Several authors I know dictate while they take the dog for a walk or ride the bus. Other authors manage to dictate while they drive. Personally, this is *not* a strategy I recommend as dictation takes a fair amount of concentration, which you should be using to drive. At any rate, whether you transcribe or dictate into your computer, a good noise-canceling microphone is an essential investment.

Chapter 3

The Options

Dragon®
Let's Make Sure We're on the Same Page

Before I talk about specific versions of Dragon®, the most effective brand of voice recognition software currently available, I need to talk about Nuance's recommendation for minimum equipment. I won't go as far as saying they're delusional — but in my estimation, their recommendations aren't rooted in the real world. Perhaps their products really will run on computers with those specifications, but as a long-time user, I remain skeptical. Most current basic configurations won't run smoothly on a computer with as little as 2 GB of RAM (as they suggest for some of their programs).

Am I a computer scientist? Heck no! I have a Doctorate Degree in Jurisprudence and my undergraduate degree is in Psychology. However, I use this technology day in and day out. For optimal speed, I would not recommend using Dragon® NaturallySpeaking or Dragon® Dictate on a machine with less than 16 GB of RAM if you want to get any amount of serious work done — especially if you want to use it in conjunction with another software program. Can it be run on less? Of course. I have a MacBook with 8 GB of RAM and it functions fine. It's not speedy, but it works.

While we're talking about basic assumptions, for purposes of clarity in this book I'm going to be referring to the most recent releases of Dragon® NaturallySpeaking and Dragon® Dictate. At the time of writing, this means Dragon® Professional Individual 15.3 and Dragon® Professional individual for Mac 6.0.8. First, this makes things easier for me as the author and you as the reader because Nuance® has had a bit of an identity crisis when it comes to brand identity and they keep renaming their products. It's nearly impossible to keep them all straight.

For purposes of clarity, I will refer to these products as Dragon® NaturallySpeaking, and Dragon® Dictate — even though currently the product names are similar. Additionally, there are many versions out there. Do you absolutely have to have the latest version? Of course not. If you're running Windows 8, Dragon® NaturallySpeaking 13 Premium is a perfectly acceptable product. On the other hand, older versions of Dragon® Dictate tend to be a little more problematic.

Becoming an author is an interesting journey. It is one of the few professions you can enter with little or no investment. In theory, all you need to get started is a pencil and a pad of paper and a good imagination. It's true. You can make a minimal investment in your career as an author, but that doesn't mean it's optimal for you. As we've already discussed, there are risks of repetitive stress injury, injuries to your neck and back, and strain on your eyes. As an author, your primary asset is you. You need to stay healthy. That means you need a quality chair, a good monitor, a reliable computer and the proper software.

I understand the struggle you're having with yourself. Almost everything we do as authors is expensive. Take heart! Voice recognition software is much cheaper than it used to be. Still, there are some places where you can't really skimp when you enter this arena. Much as I hate to admit it, every time I fork over money for a new upgrade (and trust me when I tell you it's been thousands over the course of thirty years), the software gets better with each upgrade. You need a computer with sufficient memory and processing power, and you need a quality microphone. Just as a carpenter would not go into business with just a hammer and a few penny nails or an accountant would never dream of hanging a shingle without having the latest in accounting and tax preparation software, we as authors have to arm ourselves with the tools we need to succeed.

I'll also assume you're familiar with the operating system of your computer and whatever word processing program you choose to use. For example, I might say the keyboard shortcut for paste is **COMMAND + V** on a Mac or **CONTROL + V** on a Windows computer. I don't speak computer geek fluently, so I'll be giving some tips I've learned along the way as a user of voice recognition software, but this is by no means a programming book.

For clarity, I will try to use some standard conventions. It is a little difficult because Dragon® NaturallySpeaking and Dragon® Dictate operate differently. However, I will try to communicate commands consistently. For example, when I talk about a command I want you to speak, such as, **Correct That**, I'll put it in **bold.** If you need to pause briefly when you give a command I will use a comma. For example, **Caps On**, [followed by the rest of your text], **Caps Off.** In this instance, you need to pause briefly before typing your text that you want capitalized and before proceeding with uncapitalized text.

If I am referring to a shortcut on your computer such as **FUNCTION + F11** to toggle your microphone on and off on a Mac, I will use ALLCAPS and **bold.**

Sometimes, a command will have options. I will indicate those like this: **Format That** <font> I will put the option in italics like *Garamond Regular.*

Occasionally, I'll talk about commands which will require input from you. I will refer to the text you are changing like this: **Correct** [misrecognized text].

Now that we've gotten all the assumptions out of the way, let's talk about your options within voice recognition software, shall we?

Dragon® NaturallySpeaking

Dragon® NaturallySpeaking is the most common line of voice recognition products now owned by Nuance®.

Currently, the NaturallySpeaking line has two products: Dragon® Professional Individual and Dragon® Home 15. To avoid product confusion, Nuance® has phased out its Premium line, although you can still find it for sale at many retail outlets.

The Legal Edition and Medical Edition are specialty versions of Dragon® Professional Individual. They use the same speech engine, but they both have specialized vocabularies which are much larger. Additionally, the medical version is designed to work seamlessly with all major EHR platforms. The Legal Version allows you to easily dictate things like section symbols or difficult case citations. Many frequently cited cases are standard in the vocabulary — but unless you specialize in bankruptcy or appellate law, you probably don't need to incur the additional expense.

Dragon® Home 15 may be appropriate for some simple tasks like writing letters and dictating memos. However, it is a stripped-down version of the program. It is missing some key functions and capabilities you'll need as an author. For example, it lacks the ability to transcribe or customize your vocabulary. Comparing Dragon® Home 15 to Dragon® Individual Professional is a little like comparing Microsoft WordPad to the full version of Microsoft Word. Although you can create a document on both programs, your experience will be vastly different.

If you want to take a baby step and try the Home version before you pay for the full version of Dragon® Professional Individual, older versions of Home Edition Dragon® NaturallySpeaking are usually inexpensive. I've seen the program for sale at online retailers and other stores such as Walmart and OfficeMax for under forty dollars.

If you don't mind using older technology, Dragon® NaturallySpeaking Premium 13 may be sufficient for your needs. It utilizes a slightly less accurate speech model than Dragon® Individual Professional 15 — but even so, it is still amazingly accurate. Just be aware that you are purchasing a product with obsolescence already built-in. As operating systems continue to improve, there won't be updates or patches available because Nuance® has announced they will be discontinuing support for Dragon® NaturallySpeaking 13 in January of 2019.

One substantial advantage Dragon® NaturallySpeaking has over its counterpart on the Mac side is that it learns very efficiently from corrected mistakes. Dragon® Dictate has distinct difficulties with this task. Over time, your profile should become more accurate rather than less. I will have more on proper profile maintenance later on.

Dragon® Professional Individual 15 is the most sophisticated, advanced version currently available. It's also the most flexible. Some users have reported better than ninety-nine percent accuracy right out of the box. Personally, my numbers are closer to ninety-seven percent accuracy. Sometimes my cerebral palsy can cause my speech to be a bit slurred. It has been my experience that voice recognition software in general tends to do better with men's voices. My husband and two boys have always been able to get better accuracy straight out of the box than I can. Dragon® Professional Individual 15 also allows you to have both customized words and commands. I will explain to you later how I use this capacity to speed up my writing.

The Professional version allows you to sync with Dragon® Anywhere. This is handy if you replace your profiles often.

It's hard to lay out the differences between the earlier versions of Dragon® NaturallySpeaking and Dragon® Professional Individual 15 without whipping out charts, graphs, and computer speak. Here's what I can tell you about how the improvements will impact you on a practical level: The new versions, both on Windows and Mac, are faster with less lag time and have more tolerance of background noise. Earlier versions of voice recognition software would interpret virtually every small noise as a word. This meant that if you exhaled with any degree of force or someone in the next room laughed, Dragon® would place interesting words in your document. Don't get me wrong, sometimes it still happens, but it occurs less with the newest versions.

If you install a new version of your voice recognition software, start with a fresh profile and import your custom vocabulary words.

Fighting lag when you're trying to get words on the page is very frustrating. Assuming you have an adequate amount of RAM and processing power, Dragon® Professional Individual 15 does an admirable job of keeping up. You can help with this by closing any programs you are not actively using while you are dictating. Dragon® is a resource-hungry program.

Although it is possible to preserve your profiles when you upgrade to a newer version of Dragon® NaturallySpeaking, I don't recommend doing so. Instead, you should export your custom vocabulary words (before you upgrade), save them on an external drive and import them into your new profile once you have installed your new software. I will describe how to export your custom vocabulary words a little later.

Dragon® Dictate

If you use a Mac, Nuance® has one option for you: Dragon® Dictate. Once again, they've had difficulty settling on a name, but the most recent version of the name is Dragon® Professional Individual for Mac. (For purposes of simplicity in this book, I will continue to refer to Dragon® Professional Individual 6.0.8 as Dragon® Dictate to avoid confusion with the Windows product.)

If you were to do a quick Internet search about Dragon® Dictate 6.0, you might come away with the impression that it is a completely unusable product. This is simply not the case.

I own Dragon® Dictate 6.0.8, Dragon® Professional Individual 15.3 and Dragon® Anywhere. I also own Scrivener and Microsoft Word for all three platforms. My Windows computer and my MacBook Pro are roughly equivalent machines with almost identical specs. Given those facts, you might be curious about which platform I choose to use to dictate every day. My answer might surprise you with all you may have read or heard about Dragon® Dictate. I dictate every day on my MacBook Pro using Dragon® Dictate 6.0.8 and Scrivener 3.

There are others who vehemently insist Dragon® NaturallySpeaking is such a vastly superior product it deserves its own dedicated computer or modification to the operating system on the Mac to run both Windows and OS. I respectfully disagree.

For Mac fans, I can tell you all hope is not lost. Although there are features available on Dragon® NaturallySpeaking which I prefer, for the most part, I find the products to be relatively equal. There are some things I can do on my Mac with Dragon® Dictate 6.0.8 that I cannot do with Dragon® NaturallySpeaking and Windows.

Typically, I publish about eight books per year; this equates to about seven hundred thousand words. I choose to dictate using my MacBook Pro, Yeti by Blue Mic, and Dragon® 6.0.8 with Scrivener 3. This is my favorite combination. I like the features of Scrivener 3 because I can dictate directly into the program without having to copy and paste. For me personally, the act of copying and pasting disrupts my creative process.

So, if the products don't have an appreciable difference in quality, why does the Mac version continue to get maligned? I think it's a combination of factors. First, Dragon® Dictate acts differently than Dragon® NaturallySpeaking. Even with all of my experience with voice recognition software, it was a little bit of a learning curve for me to make the move over to Dragon® Dictate. Secondly, they have had a series of bad launches. There are consistent quality issues which tend to plague the entire Dragon® Dictate line, regardless of which version you use. For whatever reason, the programmers at Nuance® haven't been able to resolve some of the glitches which date back to the time when Dragon® Dictate was known as MacSpeech. This is incredibly frustrating for long-time users and newcomers alike.

I'm not privy to what happens inside the research labs at Nuance®. I wish I was. Had they consulted long-term users like myself who dictate hundreds of thousands of words every year, we could've told them version 6.0 was not ready for prime time when they released it. Sadly, they did not. Consequently, they unleashed a nightmare. Fortunately, they've been able to fix most of the problems and — for the most part — it's stable now. Make no mistake; despite the newfound similarities between the names, the products on the Windows platform and the Mac platform seemingly bear little resemblance to each other. They don't share similar roots on a programming level and they operate differently. Although I've been assured by people in the know that the speech engines are nearly identical, my personal experience tells me they operate quite differently.

I won't hide the ball; I freely admit that in some areas, Dragon® NaturallySpeaking is a stronger product when compared side-by-side with Dragon® Dictate. I have been using Dragon® Dictate for over four years. During that time, the quality gap between the two products has narrowed substantially. However, there are still noticeable deficiencies.

From an accuracy standpoint, in my opinion, both products perform equally. Dragon® Dictate recognizes speech phenomenally well. On my MacBook Pro with 16 GB of RAM, it is lightning quick. It's not too shabby on my older MacBook Pro with 8 GB of RAM either. It is noticeably slower on my older Mac mini which also has 8 GB of RAM.

Like most programs on the Mac, installation is straightforward and set up is painless. Unfortunately, the rest of what I have to say about Dragon® Dictate is going to sound like an unending list of criticisms. It's not intended to be; it's just that some of Dragon® Dictate's features could use some work under the hood that I'm not capable of doing as an end user. Whenever possible, I'll give you my best work-around tips.

Sometimes a feature will not be a flaw, but rather something I used to do in Dragon® NaturallySpeaking that I wish I could do in Dragon® Dictate.

Let's get the bad news out of the way first. Dragon® Dictate for Mac is prone to crashing. It doesn't crash as often as it used to, but in my opinion, it melts down at an unacceptably high rate for a commercially available program in its sixth version. But, what do I know? I'm only an end-user. Fortunately, it rarely takes the other programs with it. I will give more in depth troubleshooting tips later in the book, but the easiest way to deal with unexpected crashes of Dragon® Dictate is to run the Activity Monitor (a built-in utility within your operating system on the Mac). Simply **Force Quit** Dragon® Dictate and then **Restart** the program.

The other major glitch within Dragon® Dictate for Mac is its inability to keep its place within your document. There are various explanations as to why this happens. Some people theorize it occurs when you touch your keyboard. The program keeps a cache of your previously dictated words to facilitate editing. The interference from another input device is thought to disrupt the way the program operates. Personally, I've noticed difficulties when Dragon® misinterprets a command such as *Correct That.*

Whatever the cause, this glitch can be incredibly frustrating. Not only does it send your cursor racing through your document to find some mysterious text known only to the program, it sometimes deletes random words, leaving a mysterious alphabet code (a.k.a. Dragon® poop) behind when you try to dictate your next sentence.

If this happens to you, take a deep breath. It's all fixable. First, take a moment to take a sip of coffee or soda. Wait for the cursor to stop. If you notice it has deleted text, simply press **COMMAND + Z** to recover the lost text. After your text has been restored, say the command *Cache Document.* This command resets the data Dragon® has stored for what you have just dictated and corrects the problem of random letters and numbers appearing when you try to dictate.

Technically, you can correct your mistakes by selecting the word or phrase Dragon® did not recognize correctly. If you do this, it is preferable to do so with your voice. In the correction window, you simply choose the number which is closest to what you meant to say and then say **EDIT [#]**. When you have corrected the option to what you would like it to be (you may use the **SPELL** command for this), simply say **CHOOSE [#]**.

Correcting your mistakes with your voice is considered best practice and will improve your profile over time. In total candor, with Dragon® Dictate for Mac, I don't bother. I find that, unlike Dragon® NaturallySpeaking, Dragon® Dictate doesn't learn particularly well from correction.

Dragon® Dictate for Mac is accurate enough out of the box that if I'm having trouble with accuracy, I simply save my customized words and commands and start over with a new profile.

You can transcribe with Dragon® Dictate. The process is quite painless in Dragon® Professional Individual 6.0.8. You may have heard that you can't train Dragon® Dictate to transcribe more accurately as you can Dragon® NaturallySpeaking. This notion is inaccurate. You can. The process is simply different than it is in Dragon® NaturallySpeaking.

At this point, you're probably scratching your head and asking yourself why I made the switch to the Mac version. It's a fair question, given the limitations of Dragon® Dictate. For me personally, it became a balancing act. I had to choose between the functionality of Scrivener for Mac and the limitations of Dragon® Dictate. For several years, I've been waiting to see whether Dragon® Dictate would catch up to Dragon® NaturallySpeaking before Scrivener for Windows would catch up to Scrivener for Mac. It's an awkward place to be. Ideally, for the author in us all, both programs will make vast improvements, and everyone will be happy.

Dragon® Anywhere

If you are a fan of writing on a tablet such as your iPad, iPhone, or Android phone or tablet, there is a program for mobile devices from Nuance®. It is called Dragon® Anywhere. There is a lot to like about this program. Unlike other speech-to-text applications, there is no limit to the amount you can dictate in one stretch.

Recent improvements to Dragon® Anywhere have made the interface respond more like Dragon® NaturallySpeaking and Dragon® Dictate; you can now select a word and correct it. This was a much-needed improvement. You can also train words and add vocabulary words.

One of my favorite features is the ability to save vocabulary words across all of your platforms. If you make changes to your vocabulary within Dragon® Anywhere and you own Dragon® Dictate 6.0.8 or Dragon® Professional Individual 15, your custom vocabulary can be synced. This is especially handy if you are like me and you replace your profile often.

Sounds cool, right? However, there are some significant downsides to Dragon® Anywhere. Chief among them is its price. It is a subscription-based product and currently costs fifteen dollars a month or one hundred and fifty dollars per year. For the average user, I'm not sure it's worth the investment. Dragon® Anywhere has other limitations I find bothersome for such an expensive piece of software. For example, it is still unacceptably difficult to make corrections if the word you want to use is not one of the options Dragon® has chosen. Secondly, even though Microsoft Office has had its suite of programs available for mobile devices for years, Dragon® Anywhere does not work within those programs. It also doesn't work directly with the iOS version of Scrivener. This seems like a major oversight.

If you want high levels of productivity and you want to be mobile, my recommendation is to look toward transcription. On paper, Dragon® Anywhere seems like a great idea, but in my experience, it's not very practical to use.

Other voice recognition software programs

Google Docs and Siri

For people who are serious about using dictation as a tool to produce words every day, in my opinion Dragon® is the only option worth considering. Okay, okay stop throwing things at your reading device or computer. I promise I'll explain.

I am aware there are other options out there. I've actually used most of them. I've invested thousands of dollars in the past thirty years on voice recognition software. I swear, I'd love to find a less expensive option. If Apple or Microsoft would build an equivalent into their operating systems, I would be celebrating in the street. Unfortunately, my dream hasn't come true just yet.

There have been some valiant attempts. For example, Google Docs introduced text-to-speech capabilities a couple of years ago. The accuracy is pretty good. Many authors I know love to use Google Docs because it's easy to collaborate on projects and you can work on your projects on any device anywhere and access them any place you have Wi-Fi access. Unfortunately, it has some real shortfalls — for example, the lack of basic punctuation. I'm not talking about esoteric things like section symbols or ampersands. I mean colons, apostrophes and quotation marks. It is possible to go back and add punctuation, but it's a pain to do — especially when you're talking about a manuscript which might be over a hundred thousand words long.

Siri has decent accuracy, but it is difficult to dictate more than a few words at a time. It is a fine tool for dictating short messages, like texts and short email messages. However, I haven't found a mechanism to be able to use it effectively for dictating long passages.

Mac OS

The Mac OS has dictation built right in and it's compatible with most programs. Dictation using the Mac OS speech software is a bit less accurate. However, it seems to have improved under High Sierra. It is more difficult to correct errors because when you select a word, there isn't a menu of options to choose from. This slows the dictation process down immensely. At least the software built into the operating system has a full complement of punctuation options, including commas, colons, semicolons and apostrophes.

Although the error rate is higher with the Mac operating system, the primary advantage is it comes preinstalled on your Mac computer. It also works directly with Scrivener, Pages and Microsoft Word.

Using the operating system is a good choice if you are merely evaluating whether dictation is going to work for you as an author. The fact that it is free with the Mac operating system makes it ideal for this purpose. However, if you try this, please don't be discouraged if your accuracy is not as high as you would like it to be. I routinely achieve a ninety-seven percent accuracy rate with Dragon® Dictate. When I switch to the Mac OS, my accuracy falls to around eighty-four percent. That may not seem like such a big drop until you consider most of my books are around seventy-thousand words each. When you are editing seventy-thousand words, that is an additional nine thousand one hundred words to correct, in addition to the other run-of-the-mill corrections I make as an author. I don't know about you, but I'm not willing to fix nine thousand more mistakes simply for the convenience of a free product.

The Windows operating system has offered its own voice recognition software option for several years. I was encouraged when I read it had been updated with Windows 10 to operate on the same engine which runs Cortana. I had not used this program in several years and I expected major improvements. Sadly, I was disappointed.

My first barrier was getting Windows 10 to recognize my microphones. It took a call to technical support to get Windows 10 to recognize my Raspberry by Blue Mic. I had better luck with my Yeti (also by Blue Mic), although it took me a couple of tries and more than a few cuss words.

After I finally got my Dell Computer which has 16 GB of RAM and an i7 Intel processor to recognize my Yeti microphone, I set up the Speech Recognition program within Windows 10.

I spent quite some time trying to dictate. Although the speech recognition program within Windows has a full complement of punctuation — unlike Google Docs — the accuracy is abysmal. The best I got was sixty-five percent.

Incidentally, when I reported my findings to my teenage son, who typically has better accuracy with voice recognition applications than I do, he was not surprised. He reports his XBox uses the same speech engine and that he obtains terrible recognition there as well.

On the plus side, the speech recognition software on your Windows 10 computer is free. However, realistically speaking, it isn't very effective for anything other than short email messages or posting on social media. If you were writing a seventy-thousand word manuscript, a sixty-five percent accuracy rate would translate into twenty-six thousand, two hundred and fifty errors caused by your voice recognition software on top of regular editing. To me, that's just not a workable statistic if you want to be a productive author.

Now that we've discussed the optimal type of software to purchase for your needs, we need to talk about the other factors involved to produce the best environment for dictation.

Chapter 4

The Rest of the Setup

Making It All Work

I can't tell you the number of conversations I've had with people who are disappointed when they start to use voice recognition software. Usually the conversations start out a little like this, "I don't know what I'm doing wrong. I read about voice recognition software and I installed it on my computer, but it just doesn't work for me. I'm really disappointed because it was expensive too!"

I always cringe a little because I know my next words are likely to give them even more heartburn. Although Nuance® does a good job of selling their product, they don't do a great job of conveying that their software alone isn't enough. The advice I'm about to give is applicable whether you use Dragon® or one of the other options such as the operating system on your computer or Google Docs.

In addition to voice recognition software, you need three other things.

1.) You need a quality microphone.

2.) You need a computer with enough processing power and memory.

3.) You need a relatively quiet dictating environment.

I'll address these each separately, but together they make up the team that allows whatever program you're using to function appropriately. If you're missing one component, it will be harder. Can you still make it work? Probably. Your accuracy may not be as high, or your system may have an unacceptable lag as it tries to compensate. In short, you'll be happier with your experience with voice recognition software if you can optimize your microphone, your computer system and your environment.

The Microphone

I've owned lots of microphones over the past thirty years. I have a box in my garage which serves as a graveyard for old microphones. It contains everything from cheap lapel microphones to expensive seven-hundred-dollar microphones designed exclusively for voice recognition and everything in between. I think I've tried virtually every type available. I have headsets, desktop mics, wireless microphones, lapel microphones, microphones which clip over one ear, some which hook over both ears, and even some designed to switch back and forth with the telephone. I can tell you what works and what doesn't work quite so well.

Ironically, some of the worst mics I've ever worked with are the ones Dragon® packages with their software. I used to assume that if Dragon® took the time to pair a microphone with their product, there must be something unique about it which makes it especially effective for dictation. I'm less gullible these days. If you're given a choice, don't bother to buy the version of Dragon® with the microphone included. It's not worth the added cost. Buy your microphone separately — you'll have a better selection.

Nuance® has a list of "approved" microphones. In my opinion, you can completely ignore this list, as it is outdated. Many of the microphones listed are not even currently available. Knowbrainer. com is a premier distributor of adaptive equipment and voice recognition software. They've been in the industry a long time and have comprehensive guides which rank microphones on many criteria.

Personally, I recommend a USB microphone with the ability to set your gain (the amount of sound the microphone hears). Wireless technology is handy, but in my experience, the quality of sound from the microphones is just not consistent enough for dictation.

In my family, we are a multiple microphone household. Each of us has our favorite mics. My favorite microphone is the Yeti by Blue Mic. It is, without exception, the best microphone I have ever used. On the other hand, my husband prefers his Snowball by Blue Mic. Our son likes his Samson Go Mic because it's compact and clips to the edge of his laptop. When I was in the hospital last year for nearly a month, I enjoyed the convenience of my Raspberry by Blue Mic. Even though it's a small microphone, it had almost the same accuracy as my full-size mic. I like the fact that I am able to adjust the gain. It was handy to have so much control in a noisy environment like the hospital.

No matter which microphone you choose, there are some things to remember. Some microphones work best if they are right up against your mouth. Others work better if you are a few inches away. Make sure you experiment and determine which settings work best for your individual microphone. Once you've determined what distance is appropriate for your microphone, try to stay consistent. Varying the distance between your mouth and the microphone can cause a large discrepancy in your accuracy.

It is a good idea to have a foam or fuzzy cover on your microphone. Dragon® can do interesting things with puffs of air from your speech. In my case, it is particularly fond of turning them into "'s" when I least expect them. If you are using a desktop mic like a Yeti by Blue Mic, a pop filter can help protect your microphone and improve your accuracy.

When you set up a microphone, it's a good idea to check and see what your microphone is hearing in your environment. I like to use a third-party app for this. Audacity is a free app, and it is available for both Windows and Mac. It looks complicated, but you don't need to use all of its complex features to test whether your microphone is receiving sound properly.

To use the Audacity tool, simply record a snippet of your voice. It doesn't need to be long — a few seconds will do. Look at the tracings of the recording. If the wavelengths are completely flat, it means your microphone is not getting enough sound from you. You need to turn up your gain or sit closer to the microphone. On the other hand, if the wavelengths are so wide they are covering the entire graph, your microphone is receiving too much sound and your speech will be distorted. The sound will be clipped and Dragon® will not be able to understand your speech. You need to turn down the gain on your microphone or move away from the microphone. Perhaps you will need to do both. Ideally, your sound waves appear like the graphics on the bottom. There is movement with your speech, but it is not drastic, and it is not going off the charts.

Once you have found the ideal position and gain setting for your microphone, make sure you save your microphone as the default microphone for your computer.

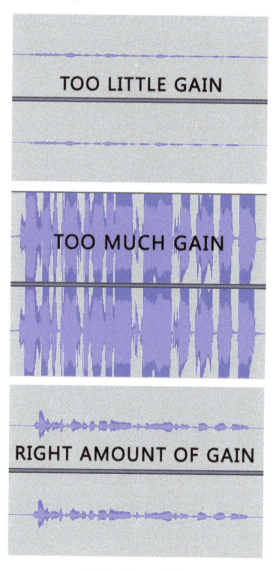

Setting Proper Gain

There are other things which can affect the performance of your microphone. I have had USB cords break down on a pretty regular basis. Additionally, well-meaning, but fidgety family members have been known to change the input settings on my microphone. This led to an inexplicable decline in my accuracy. I took all sorts of unnecessary draconian steps including wiping out my entire profile before I finally discovered what the problem actually was.

If you strongly prefer a wireless microphone, Knowbrainer recommends the Sennheiser PRESENCE UC Bluetooth Headset.

You may have an older microphone with the dual plugs designed to go in the microphone port and earphone port of your computer. If your computer is one of the newer models, you may not even have these ports. If that is the case, you can purchase a USB converter. You might want to consider this anyway; it can improve the performance of your microphone and bypass your sound card.

Additionally, if you use a desktop microphone like the Yeti, I recommend using a boom arm rather than setting it on your desk. Desktop microphones can be very sensitive to vibrations on your desk. When you use your mouse and keyboard, your microphone can pick up the vibrations and deposit strange characters in your manuscript.

It is important to note when you set up an external microphone on a MacBook, MacBook Pro or MacBook Air, you need to go into your preferences and turn down the volume on the internal microphone. If you fail to do this, your internal microphone will be competing with your USB microphone.

In the graphic below, you can see I have the internal microphone turned down as far as it will go, and my Yeti microphone turned up to seventy-five percent. Additionally, I choose to show my sound preferences on the menu bar.

Just a quick reminder: anytime you change your microphone or your environment, you need to rerun your microphone set up within Dragon®. The good news is that these days, it's no longer an arduous process; it only takes a few seconds. If it takes longer than that, there is likely an issue with your setup. Your gain probably isn't turned up high enough on your microphone, there's a problem with your USB cord, your microphone is shut off or the microphone you have chosen isn't set up as your default device.

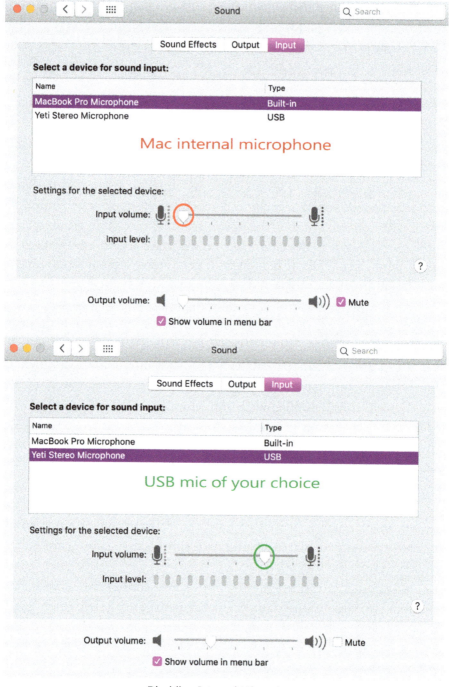

Disabling Internal Microphone

While dictating this book, my accuracy suddenly took a dive. I went through my usual troubleshooting processes and replaced all my cables, checked my settings and even reinstalled my program (several times) all to no avail. For some unknown reason, my microphone failed. I was fortunate because I had an extended warranty and was able to replace my microphone. Once I replaced my Yeti, everything was back to normal.

I learned two things from the experience. First, it doesn't matter how much you spend on a microphone, when you put as many hours of use on a piece of equipment as I do, it can malfunction. Secondly, when you invest money in an expensive microphone, it's a good idea to buy a warranty.

As good as your microphone may be, it's not the only component involved. You also need an adequate computer to run the software.

The Computer

In order for any voice recognition software program to run properly, it must have a computer with enough processing power to run it. This is probably the area which frustrates me the most about the marketing information Nuance® puts out regarding their software. If you were to read the recommendations on their packaging, you might assume you could get away with as few as 4 GB of RAM. While Dragon® might load under those conditions, I can assure you, you would drive yourself crazy trying to operate under those conditions. Although it's technically possible, I don't recommend trying to run Dragon® Dictate or Dragon® NaturallySpeaking on a computer with anything less than 8 GB of RAM and I recommend 16 GB of RAM. I have a MacBook Pro with 8 GB of RAM. The lag is noticeable compared to my other MacBook Pro, which has 16 GB of RAM.

Whichever version of Dragon® you decide to use, it is a memory intensive program. You can help yourself out by closing programs you are not actively using. Dragon® saves your speech files in a cache file. In Dragon® NaturallySpeaking, you can adjust the amount of memory you dedicate to this. You can also decide whether you want to save a record of your dictated speech with your files when you save your file. If you are running low on storage space, you may want to evaluate how important this feature is to you. Sometimes when you are editing, it is helpful to hear what you actually said versus what Dragon® thought you said. Unfortunately, this feature is not an option in Dragon® Dictate. Although you can ask for a read back, it is not in your voice, it is the automated computer voice you set up within the operating system.

Processing speed and the type of hard drive you have will also impact your experience with voice recognition software. A solid-state drive works better than others and an i7 processor or equivalent works well.

I recommend a high amount of RAM and a quick processor for good reason. That's not to say Dragon® won't run on less powerful equipment. I know some authors who report happily running Dragon® NaturallySpeaking on a Microsoft Surface. They love the portability. Just be aware Dragon® NaturallySpeaking will not work on a Chromebook or a computer running Windows RT.

If you have to run Dragon® on a less powerful computer, you can mitigate the impact by dictating into TextEdit or WordPad. These programs have a very small footprint and consume small amounts of processing power in addition to what Dragon® uses. Additionally, fancy screensavers, running your email or task managing software or social media in the background can also eat up your resources.

Your Environment

Environment frequently gets overlooked when it comes to the role it plays in optimal dictation. Small noises can degrade the quality of your dictation. A few years ago, Oregon had a particularly hot spell and our ancient, overworked heat pump wasn't cutting it, so I was supplementing it with our ceiling fan. I didn't think much of it, but my accuracy took a complete nose dive. When I complained about this to my husband and pondered whether I needed to replace my favorite microphone, he pointed to the ceiling fan and asked the obvious question. Sure enough, when I ran the microphone set up again, this time running the microphone set up with the ceiling fan in the background, my accuracy increased. I could never get it back to the levels it was without the ceiling fan running, but it was pretty close.

Recent versions of Dragon® do a good job of screening out superfluous noise. That is, if the noise is present when you run your microphone set up. So, if you plan to have a TV or radio running in the background when you are dictating, make sure that this is the environment you replicate when you run your set up. Having said that, I do recommend your environment be as quiet as possible for dictation. I recognize it is not always feasible; just do the best you can. If your environment changes, you need to rerun your microphone set up.

When you are choosing a location to dictate, try to avoid places where there are sharp noises such as cupboards opening and closing or a lot of people coming in and out of rooms. Area rugs can cut down on the sound of footfalls on wood floors. We have laminated floors in our home and I can always tell when my dogs need to go in for a grooming session by how often their nails click on the floor. Again, make sure the gain on your microphone is set as low as possible. If the gain is set too high on your microphone, too many extraneous sounds will be picked up

If you can't be in a quiet environment, sometimes you can create one through the use of a sound booth. Amazon has several decent options for around one hundred and fifty dollars — professional versions cost closer to two thousand dollars. You can assemble your own from a presentation trifold (available at most office supply stores) and an egg crate mattress topper (available at any large chain store). Simply use adhesive or double-sided tape to adhere the pieces of foam mattress to the presentation board.

If you dictate in radically different environments, I recommend having a different profile for each. For example, when I worked outside my home, I had an office profile and a home profile. The acoustics were just too different for me to manage in one profile.

A word about internal noise: it can be extremely detrimental to your accuracy. Dragon® is a memory intensive program. This is especially true if you run it with another program like Microsoft Word. It is taxing on your computer and can cause it to overheat. Don't use your laptop on your lap with blankets — use a lap desk with a hard surface (preferably one with a built-in, quiet fan). Amazon has several which run off battery power. Many of them conveniently have extra USB ports. To reduce the amount of time the internal fan runs on my MacBook Pro, which I utilize more like a desktop, I have it sitting on a wire cooling rack (like the ones you use to cool baked goods). It sits away from me and I use a wireless keyboard and trackpad.

We've laid the groundwork for a great set up, you've got a spot-on microphone, a solid computer system and a conducive environment for dictation, now it's time to start setting up for success. I've divided the next section into two parts — one for NaturallySpeaking and the other for Dragon® Dictate.

Chapter 5

Getting Started
Working with Dragon® NaturallySpeaking

Installation

When you first get Dragon® NaturallySpeaking, it can seem pretty daunting to install. So, even though most of you probably already have the software, I'm going to take a moment to talk about the installation process for those of you who are new to the program.

First, you need to install your microphone on your computer. Make sure it is the default input device. If you are running Windows 10, you may need to boost the audio capabilities of your USB microphone. I will address this in the troubleshooting section.

If you are a student or an educator and you have access to an email account with an .edu extension or can otherwise document your status, it is sometimes (but not always) cheaper to get the educational version of Dragon® NaturallySpeaking. If you've elected to go with the Student/Teacher version, you will need to register your software using this email address and you will need access to this account.

If you have registered software previously with Nuance®, it is helpful to have your email address and password available. It just makes the process go more smoothly.

If you purchased a disk copy of your software, it will come with some stickers containing your serial number. You should do two things: Take a Sharpie and write the serial number on the disc and email yourself a copy of the serial number. (Yes, it is that important.)

Digital copies purchased directly from Nuance® or from other online stores will have a copy of the serial number on the receipt. Again, back this up and keep it in a safe place.

If you purchase an upgrade copy of your software, you need the serial number of your previous version of Dragon® to activate your product. You can still install the new product, but the number of times you can launch it will be limited before you have to activate it. If you have purchased previous versions of Dragon® from Nuance®, they have a tool on their site which will allow you to look up your previous orders from Digital River. You will need to know the email address you used and your password.

I recommend you close all the programs you have running, including all the programs you run in the background. This includes your antivirus program. Dragon® is notorious for having conflicts with antivirus software while it is being installed. For your own sanity, have a good movie queued up or a book you've been dying to read nearby because Dragon® is a big program. It takes a while to install. This is especially true if you choose to download the program. It is best not to be doing something else with your computer during the installation process. The program may look like it's doing nothing or — even worse — like it's completely stalled for several minutes at a time. Even though I have installed several versions of Dragon®, it still takes me off guard when this happens. Chances are, you haven't done anything wrong, it just takes time.

After your product has installed, it will ask you for the serial number. This will either be on the sticker attached to the protective jacket on the CD or on your receipt which came with your downloaded copy. If you have the upgrade version, you will also need the serial number of your previous version. If you have not already registered with Nuance®, you will be asked to do so. This is a good idea because it will help you keep track of serial numbers and makes it easier to ask for support in the future.

After you have installed your product, make sure you check for updates. Nuance® frequently releases patches and updates to their products to fix glitches and to make their products as compatible as they can. At the time I am writing this book, the current version of Dragon® Professional Individual for Windows is 15.3.

Profiles

After you've installed your product, the first thing Dragon® will ask you to do is set up a profile. Make sure you're using the microphone you intend to use, and the environment is representative of how it will be when you are dictating. Choose a name you will be able to find on your computer. This may seem silly, but when I am running multiple computers, my profiles might look a little something like this:

- Mary MacBook Pro
- Mary Dell
- Mary with a cold MacBook Pro

When you have your profiles backed up to a flash drive, you'll want to make sure you can tell them apart.

You will be asked to choose a vocabulary size. In general, this defaults to the largest size. I usually leave this setting alone. The only reason to change this is if your computer is extremely light on memory.

The next step is to choose a country. On my version of Dragon® Pro Individual 15.3, I chose to only install the vocabulary from the United States to save space on my hard drive. Therefore, my choices are limited here.

You will then be asked to choose an accent. I was raised in Oregon and I don't have a discernible accent. So, I always choose standard. For the vast majority of people, standard will be sufficient. However, if you are struggling with poor accuracy rates, you might want to play with this setting.

Women who have soft or high voices can sometimes do better if they choose the teen setting. I've had friends from the Northeast with the Boston accents who report the British accent setting works better for them. If you tend to drop off syllables at the end of your words, you might try the southern accent setting to see if it helps your accuracy.

Next, you will be asked to set up your microphone. I want you to stop and take a breath. No, literally that's what I want you to do. Several years ago, there used to be an advanced setting in Dragon® which used to show you how Dragon® calibrated the microphone setting. They no longer show you the process, but if they did, you would learn that the program needs a couple of seconds to ascertain the baseline level of the noise in your environment before you begin to speak. So, before you start to read the prepared script, pause for a couple of seconds and let the microphone listen to the background noise of your environment. Then, proceed to read the text in a natural tone. Don't try to slow down or over-enunciate your words. Just speak in a clear, deliberate voice.

If you run into difficulty setting up your profile, you might want to turn down the gain on your microphone and try again.

It doesn't hurt to try out several settings to see which is most comfortable for you. If you don't like the settings in a particular profile, you can simply delete it.

After you have listened to a snippet of your microphone setup and determined you can hear yourself, Dragon® will give you the opportunity to run through the tutorial. I recommend you do this at least once, if for no other reason than to make the program stop bothering you about running it. The tutorial offers helpful advice about using the menu, commands, and punctuation.

Training

Training Dragon® used to be a rather complicated process. These days, it's pretty accurate right out of the box. Unless you need a specialized vocabulary, you can count on Dragon® to recognize most of what you say. There are some notable exceptions.

Dragon® doesn't do particularly well with cuss words. I can understand why the programmers of Dragon® would program against including cuss words. In the business world, it's probably not appropriate to use them as often as we do on the creative side of things. However, I'm often asked how to make Dragon® swear. It can be done, usually through the use of custom vocabulary words and training Dragon® the way you speak through the Vocabulary Training tool.

Another area of weakness is homonyms. Again, this is understandable. Dragon® understands more from context. If you say the word "there" by itself, of course, the program doesn't understand which word you were intending to use. However, if you say, "It was their turn.", Dragon® is more likely to pick up the proper context. Try to use complete sentences when you dictate. The program will have an easier time determining what you meant to say.

You can increase the odds Dragon® will recognize your speech correctly by training Dragon® to adapt to the way you speak.

Dragon® will give you the option to use documents and emails to teach the program how you speak. You can elect to use this tool. But I urge you to do so with caution. It can actually erode your accuracy. Don't check the box to use your emails to improve your language model. However, you may select specific documents which are representative of your writing style to help Dragon® learn your character names and the cadence of your speech. Before you choose a document, make sure you have spell checked it and removed any odd capitalizations, email addresses or phone numbers you don't want Dragon® to remember. Although it may be tempting to choose a large volume of documents for Dragon® to process, I urge you to be selective. It will be more effective if you choose documents which are reflective of the type of writing you will be doing while you are dictating.

It can take some time for Dragon® to complete this process. Dragon® will come up with a list of words that it is not familiar with. Sometimes words will appear on the list because the capitalization is different from what Dragon® is used to. Examine this list carefully. Choose the words you want Dragon® to add to your vocabulary. Simply click add. After you've done so, Dragon® will spend some more time adjusting your profile.

Honestly, this tool is not my favorite way to improve accuracy. I have found it to be a bit counterproductive. Of course, your mileage may vary. I have found other methods to be more helpful.

This method is a little time-consuming, but it's worth it.

After you have finished setting up your profile in Dragon®, I recommend you take about five pages of your own words (or about fifteen hundred words) and dictate it. This is much more effective than reading the curated writing examples Dragon® used to provide in earlier versions of NaturallySpeaking.

You should use a low-resource program like WordPad or TextEdit for this task. Correct any misrecognized words as you go during this process. Using your voice to make corrections is best. I will cover that topic in-depth in a moment.

Yes, I am aware this is a tedious, painstaking process. However, it is also the way Dragon® learns. You need to be consistent in correcting mistakes. Fortunately, most of the time, Dragon® doesn't make many errors if you have a properly set up microphone in a quiet environment. I promise, the time you put into nurturing your profile will pay off in accuracy later on.

Correcting Mistakes Within Dragon® NaturallySpeaking

One of the most powerful things you can do to improve your accuracy when you are using Dragon® NaturallySpeaking is to correct the program when it makes a mistake.

However, it is important to draw some distinctions. The first one is to determine whether you made an error when you were speaking the words, or whether Dragon® NaturallySpeaking actually misheard what you said. You'll need to treat these types of errors very differently.

If you simply stumble over your words, or don't say what you intended to say, you have a couple of options. You can say **Scratch That** or **Undo That**. One of the nice features about Dragon® NaturallySpeaking is that editing is very easy. You can choose to delete or edit a single word, a string of words, a series of words, the last five words, or the last two paragraphs. It's really flexible. In Dragon® NaturallySpeaking, if I want to work with the paragraph above, I can say **Select [however through said]** and it will highlight the whole paragraph above. I can do anything to that paragraph — I can format it with *italics*, **bold**, or simply delete it.

This is one of the areas in which Dragon® NaturallySpeaking is much more user-friendly than Dragon® Dictate.

On the other hand, if Dragon® NaturallySpeaking made the air (like it just did there) because the word I said was error, you need to go back and correct the program and train it to recognize the word the proper way. If you catch the misrecognition right away, you can simply say **Correct That** and Dragon® will select the word and give you a list of options it believes you said. These days, Dragon® is so accurate that the correct word will very often be the second choice. This is especially true, if, like in the example above, the words are homonyms.

You can change your settings so Dragon® will show up to nine options in the Correction Box. Personally, I don't like to take the time to spell out my corrections, so I like to improve the odds that the correct version will be in the correction box.

If you don't notice the mistake until later, you can still select the misrecognized word by saying **Correct** [misrecognized text]. If you are unsure what you actually said, you can use the command **Play That Back** and Dragon® will play back the text in your own voice. However, please be aware that this command does not work if you typed the word or if you have moved the block of text around since you first dictated it.

The correction box will appear. If the correct version of what you wanted to say appears, simply say **Choose <#>** (whichever number matches the choice which is correct).

If it doesn't appear, you can say **Spell That.** Usually, after you enter the first couple of letters, your word will appear among the options. I started using voice recognition software back when the recognition part of the programming wasn't so great. So, I learned the International Radio Alphabet as a survival mechanism. Now, it is second nature to me. It can be a helpful tool because sometimes it is difficult to distinguish a D from a B. These days, Dragon® products are much more flexible than they used to be. If you want to dictate a B in the **Spell That** command, you can say *B, Letter B* or *Bravo.*

International Radio Alphabet

Letter	IRA Equivalent	Letter	IRA Equivalent
A	Alpha	N	November
B	Bravo	O	Oscar
C	Charlie	P	Papa
D	Delta	Q	Québec
E	Echo	R	Romeo
F	Foxtrot	S	Sierra
G	Golf	T	Tango
H	Hotel	U	Uniform
I	India	V	Victor
J	Juliett	W	Whiskey
K	Kilo	X	X-ray
L	Lima	Y	Yankee
M	Mike	Z	Zulu

International Radio Alphabet

You have the option to train a word you have just corrected if it is convoluted or difficult to pronounce. Training a word can be helpful if Dragon® repeatedly misrecognizes the way you say a common word. I don't know if it's an idiosyncrasy of mine, but Dragon® can't seem to understand me when I say the word mirror. Whenever I make a new profile, I always have to go in and train the pronunciation of that particular word. After struggling with the word succinctly for a while, I actually went to the Internet and asked people how they pronounced it and figured out there was a good reason Dragon® was having problems understanding me. I discovered my pronunciation was quite aberrant compared to the pool of people I polled.

Training Dragon® to respond to the way you speak individual words can cut down on your error rate. You can do this in two separate places. The training option appears in the correction window and when you add custom vocabulary words.

Occasionally, if you correct a word for which Dragon® NaturallySpeaking has a pop-up window for what it calls smart formatting, you will be presented with a couple of options. If you don't want your formatting choices in the future to reflect either of those choices simply close the box. However, if you do, for example, want to use fractions or have your numbers spelled out, simply choose the option you would like, and the next time Dragon® NaturallySpeaking encounters the same type of number or word, the program will attempt to apply the same rule.

Speaking of automatic formatting, in Dragon® NaturallySpeaking, it is possible under Tools to set your preferences so Dragon® will insert your commas and periods for you. I choose not to use this option because it can lead to some odd results if you pause in the middle of your sentence while you dictate. However, I have spoken with other authors who enjoy using this function as a safety net. So, you may want to try to see if it's helpful. If you don't care for it, you can always turn off, as I have.

Moving around your document when you use Dragon® NaturallySpeaking is relatively easy. You can move by line, by character or by word. You simply say **Move up Two Lines** or **Move Down Two Lines. Move up Four Paragraphs** or **Delete Previous Four Words.** You can use the **Undo That** to reverse your last ten actions (provided you did not do an intervening action with your keyboard).

There is one important concept I want to discuss when it comes to correcting mistakes. Please don't confuse this process with the editing process we all do as authors. Just because we make mistakes as authors, doesn't mean Dragon® is responsible for that mistake. That's what makes the playback feature so great in NaturallySpeaking. It's one of the features I really missed when I went over to Dragon® Dictate. There's nothing like the actual recording, in your own voice, to hold your feet to the fire about whether you actually said all the words you think you did. I know when I'm tired I often leave out syllables and small words that I think I dictated. I mean … I know I said them in my head but that doesn't necessarily mean they were input into my microphone. In those cases, that's a speaking error, not a Dragon® error, and it's not something I would correct. Eventually, I definitely have to edit for that, but it's not something I use the correction box in Dragon® to correct. The same is true for punctuation errors.

Now that you know how to correct your mistakes, it's time to figure out how to put Dragon® NaturallySpeaking to work.

Using Dragon® with Other Applications

Great! You've got a shiny new profile in a brand spanking new program. So now what? Your first inclination might be to use Dragon® Pad which is Dragon®'s own internal application. If Dragon® NaturallySpeaking doesn't have full compatibility with another program, it will suggest that you use Dragon® Pad.

Don't.

Okay, I know I need to provide a more detail, but I really want my words of caution to be stark and bold.

There is a good reason I caution you against using Dragon® Pad. It crashes routinely. Not just sometimes, but it melts down with frightening regularity. Unlike other issues which plague only Dragon® Dictate, the problems with Dragon® Pad are universal. If Dragon® Pad crashes, you'll lose everything. Save yourself the heartbreak and just skip it.

If you don't use Dragon® Pad, you'll need an alternative. TextEdit is available for either Mac or Windows. It is a program with a small footprint and it doesn't cause much lag on your system. You can copy, paste and save documents. However, TextEdit is not my favorite because it's difficult to customize and causes me a lot of eyestrain.

WordPad and OneNote are good options if you like working with the Microsoft interface. They do not bog down the system as much as working with the full version of Microsoft Word.

I like to dictate directly into Grammarly (a grammar checking program available for use online for free). It is quick and efficient, and it does not add lag time. Additionally, you get a bonus grammar check before you have to copy and paste your words into whatever writing application you are using. I especially like this option because it automatically saves my dictation, no matter what else happens around me. Working in Grammarly allows for full correction and control, similar to what you would get if you were working in Microsoft Word. The only downside is that Grammarly requires Wi-Fi access to work properly.

Many of you might be asking why not just dictate in Microsoft Word?

It's a fair question. Of all the word processing programs available, Dragon® is supposed to be the most compatible with Microsoft Word. In Dragon® NaturallySpeaking 13 and later versions, Nuance® claims, "Word has full text control and natural language processing abilities."

It sounds like it should work beautifully, right? Unfortunately, in my experience, the logistics of working with Microsoft Word and Dragon® at the same time is a frustrating experience at best. Both are memory-intensive programs. If you are working with a document of any substantial length, the process slows down to an intolerable crawl.

You can choose to have Dragon® launch in sleep mode at startup. This is helpful if you want to operate your computer hands-free.

If Microsoft Word is your favorite word processor and you want to work with Dragon®, I have some tips. First, if you've worked with other programs which have installed plug-ins or macros you no longer use, uninstall them. Keep your documents small. Using bullets and other graphics can bog down your dictation. Keep in mind, neither version of Dragon® works well within tables and it is not fully supported in the online version of Office 365.

When working with Microsoft Word and either version of Dragon®, it is imperative to have as few other programs running as possible. The resource drain created by the programs working together is enormous.

Many authors I know, myself included, love to use Scrivener. I'm sad to say the Windows version of Scrivener does not work well with Dragon® NaturallySpeaking. Although it is technically possible to dictate directly into Scrivener for Windows, it is nearly impossible to edit anything once you've dictated it directly into Scrivener.

My work-around when I had to work on my Windows computer, used to be to dictate directly into Grammarly and copy and paste my words into my scene in Scrivener. However, I've found a more efficient method for working with Scrivener when I use my Windows computer.

Recently, I discovered an add-in program called Speech Productivity. In short, this program is everything Dragon® Pad should be, but isn't. There are many window types available from tiny to extra-large. There are different backgrounds including transparent, and the content within the dictation boxes is fully editable. Even if Dragon® crashes for some reason, this program saves your dictation. There is a small additional cost for this plug-in, but I think it's worth it. It works for Dragon® Professional Individual on the Windows side. It does not work with Dragon® Premium products or any of the Dragon® Dictate programs. I highly recommend Speech Productivity and I hope someday the software developer will bring his software to the Mac side too.

Working with Dragon® Dictate

Installation

Compared to installing Dragon® on Windows, installing Dragon® Dictate 6.0 on your Mac computer is a piece of cake.

Make sure you've disabled any antivirus software, your security settings are unlocked in your preferences, and you don't have any other programs running in the background.

You'll need your serial number to register your product. If you bought the CD version, it will be on the disc sleeve. Take a Sharpie pen and write your serial number directly on the disk. You should email yourself a copy of the serial number. If you downloaded your version from Amazon or directly from Nuance®, it will be on your receipt.

If you purchased a Student/Teacher copy, you will need access to your email address which makes you eligible for the educational discount.

The installation process is straightforward and there is a user interface to help you through the process. After you finish installing Dragon® Dictate 6.0, make sure you update to version 6.0.8. I always suggest that people keep their software up-to-date, but this is critically important when it comes to Nuance® products. It can mean the difference between a smoothly running piece of software and something that drives you absolutely batty. The difference between Dragon® Dictate 6.0 and 6.0.8 cannot be overstated. To say it's almost as if Dragon® Dictate 6.0 was programmed by amateur programmers would be an insult to amateur programmers — but, Nuance® has made substantial progress over the last couple of years and Dragon® Dictate 6.0.8 is stable under nearly all circumstances now.

However, at the time I'm writing this book in the summer of 2018, there is a glitch in the upgrade service which strikes if you are running High Sierra. You'll need to manually update your copy of Dragon® 6.0, using the file which can be downloaded from Nuance®. (http://Nuance®.custhelp.com/app/answers/detail/a_id/26574/~/information-on-Dragon®-professional-individual-for-mac-6.0.8)

The instructions provided by Nuance® are confusing, so I'll try to clarify them here.

- Download the zip file.

- After you've unzipped it, it will produce a new Dragon® Dictate app.

- You need to rename this app Dragon® Dictate 6.0.8.

- After you've done that, drag it into your applications folder.

- Then, put the original Dragon® Dictate app in the trash. If you wish, you can put a shortcut to Dragon® Dictate 6.0.8 on your dock.

- Now, you are ready to set up your profile in Dragon® Dictate 6.0.8.

Profiles

Once again, setting up your profile is pretty straightforward.

Make sure the mic you have chosen to use is set as your default microphone in your preferences on your Mac. Additionally, if you are using a MacBook, MacBook Pro, or MacBook Air, make sure your internal microphone is set at the lowest input level possible.

Position your microphone at its optimal level and choose a name you will be able to remember when you backup your profile to an external location. Dragon® will first ask for your region and then for your accent. For the vast majority of people, an American accent is going to be the most proficient profile. However, if you are a woman with a soft voice, you might want to choose a teen profile. If Dragon® is having a difficult time understanding you, you might want to try a couple of different types of accents to see if your accuracy rate increases.

Dragon® will now set the input levels for your microphone. Take a moment to pause before reciting the prepared text. This allows the microphone to adjust to the baseline level of sound in your room before adding your voice. Years ago, their microphone calibration tool used to show this process in its advanced settings; it was helpful information to have.

Make sure any documents you choose to use for Vocabulary Training have been thoroughly checked for spelling and grammar and are representative of the type of writing you will be doing.

If you have to read the text several times through, your gain on your microphone may not be turned up enough. Simply turn it up and run the microphone set up again. You can check your sound quality with a third-party app like Audacity.

Dragon® will give you a chance to listen to a brief snippet of your voice as it heard it during the setup process. I recommend playing it back just to make sure there were no quality issues.

It never hurts to have multiple profiles. As I mentioned before, fatigue and illness affect the way my cerebral palsy impacts my life. Therefore, when I don't feel well, I use a different profile. Between my asthma and my propensity to get upper respiratory infections, some days it is amazing that Dragon® Dictate understands anything I say.

Remember, if Dragon® is struggling to understand you, you are always free to rerun your microphone setup. If your voice has changed or your environment is different, you can set up a new profile.

If you are dictating in different environments with different microphones, it is often easier to have different profiles.

Now that you've set up your profile, it's a good time to set up your preferences within Dragon®. If you're anything like me, you'll find the default settings a little frustrating.

I always set the microphone to turn off after five minutes. I don't leave it on indefinitely.

Because I write fiction, I also uncheck the box which tells Dragon® to write numbers for me. On the few occasions when I actually prefer to type numbers, I say *Numeral* followed by the number I actually want.

If you own Dragon® Anywhere, this is where you add your account information, so you can sync your vocabulary words.

You can decide whether or not Dragon® Dictate launches when you boot up your computer and whether it is off or merely asleep upon launch. (This is a handy feature if you are operating your computer hands-free). You can also change the way your interface looks by determining the number of correction choices which appear in your correction menu.

Training

I'm quite conflicted about writing this chapter. I feel as if I should write some sort of treatise regarding best practices according to the instructions provided by Nuance®.

I'm not going to do that. I presume you purchased this book because you were interested in what I have learned in thirty years of working with voice recognition technology. I promised you I would tell you how to make Dragon® work effectively for you.

This is one case where extra training just doesn't help.

In my experience, Dragon® Dictate simply doesn't learn well. So, training doesn't work.

What does work?

— Adding custom vocabulary words with custom pronunciations.

— Vocabulary Training.

Adding a custom vocabulary word is very simple. You just click on the Dragon® symbol in your menu bar and choose edit vocabulary. Click on the plus sign and type or speak in your word the way you would like it. If it is an oddly pronounced name, you may want to phonetically spell it in the Spoken Box.

Word: Maya

Spoken: My ah

?   Cancel   OK

Custom Words with Spoken Form

After you finish adding your custom vocabulary words (or anytime you add new ones), I recommend you take a few seconds to export your custom vocabulary. It's a very simple step which will save you a ton of work if your profile becomes compromised or your computer crashes. I always backup my user words to the cloud.

The first step is to select the user words within your vocabulary.

Locating User Words in the Vocabulary Editor

The next step is to highlight all the custom vocabulary words by using **COMMAND + A**. Click on the gear on the lower left corner and click on export.

Exporting User Word List From Vocabulary Editor

Then save the file with a name you will recognize. Typically, I also add the date, so I know which file is the most current. I like to save this file somewhere on an external drive in case something happens to my hard drive.

Even though I have Dragon® Anywhere and it is not strictly necessary for me to do this anymore, I still do for my own peace of mind. One of my favorite features of Dragon® Anywhere is that it automatically syncs my vocabulary words across all of my profiles.

You can further refine Dragon®'s performance by running the Vocabulary Training function.

A Word of caution about the vocabulary training: In order for it to be effective, the documents you use need to be spell checked for spelling mistakes and grammar errors. Additionally, they need to be representative of the type of writing you'll be doing with this profile. If you'll be writing steamy romance novels, you probably don't want to use your corporate marketing reports as your writing samples.

Depending upon the length of your writing samples, this process can take a little time. Do not be alarmed. It helps if your writing samples include your character names and places used in context. Additionally, if you tend to favor dialogue in your writing, using a writing sample which is also heavy in dialogue is helpful to give Dragon® Dictate a flavor of the type of documents you will be dictating.

After the Vocabulary Training has been completed and you have added any custom words, I recommend you backup your entire profile to a thumb drive or an external hard drive. I will explain more about why I recommend this in a moment.

In my experience, unless you have a heavy accent or a speech impediment, using the curated text that Dragon® Dictate 6.0.8 provides under Voice Training is not particularly helpful. However, if you do have an atypical voice, and you are having difficulty getting Dragon® to recognize your voice correctly, it might be worth your time to run through the Voice Training tools a few times to help improve your accuracy.

I'm sure my advice will be controversial. After all, it flies in the face of everything you are likely to read elsewhere. I know. I've read the same software manuals, books, websites, and watched the same videos. However, I also dictate about a million words a year between my writing, my social media posts and my private life. My physical limitations mean I use voice recognition software for everything. I've been using a Mac computer for four years. I have been through a lot of profiles. I've used three versions of Dragon® Dictate for Mac and been through countless upgrades. All told, I've used seven different microphones just in the last four years. I have a pretty good sense of what works and what doesn't.

Although I will give you detailed instructions about how to correct your profile, if you so choose, I just don't think it's worth the investment of your time. As authors, you have better things to do.

Be careful to say the CORRECT THAT command clearly and as one phrase. If Dragon® Dictate misunderstands this command, it can send your cursor racing through your document looking for the word that.

Please note this limitation only applies to the Mac side of things. I encourage you to take the time to correct incorrect words on the Windows side. Dragon® NaturallySpeaking does a good job of learning from corrected mistakes. Unfortunately, this is one of the few areas in which the Mac version and the Windows version do not have platform equality.

You might be throwing your hands up in the air in frustration right now. What good is Dragon® Dictate if it doesn't learn from mistakes? The good news is that it doesn't really have to. It's incredibly accurate right out of the box when paired with a quality microphone in a reasonably quiet environment. You can compensate for any odd phrases or character names by adding them as custom vocabulary words under Edit Vocabulary. By further customizing Dragon®'s speech engine by allowing it to learn your speech patterns through the use of Vocabulary Training, you can reach a high degree of accuracy, even without correcting mistakes.

As I've mentioned, I find the difference in accuracy between Dragon® Professional Individual for Mac 6.0.8 and Dragon® Professional Individual 15.3 for Windows to be negligible. Each product has its strengths and its weaknesses. One of the biggest strengths is where I can use Dragon® Dictate as an author—which is what we're going to talk about next.

Correcting Mistakes with Dragon® Dictate

Just because I don't recommend you spend a great deal of time correcting your mistakes in Dragon® Dictate, doesn't mean it can't be done. There are times it makes sense to correct misrecognized words in Dragon® Dictate. It helps reinforce an atypical use of a word or a specialized character name. However, I have dictated over two dozen books using Dragon® Dictate, and in my experience, it doesn't learn as quickly as Dragon® NaturallySpeaking. Don't be discouraged if the language model doesn't readily adapt to your corrections.

If you make a mistake while you are dictating, simply say **Scratch That** or **Undo That**. If Dragon® misrecognizes what you say, and you discover the mistake right away, you can say **Correct That.** Be careful to say the command clearly and as one phrase. If Dragon® Dictate misunderstands this command, it can send your cursor racing through your document looking for the word that. Sometimes it is safer to say **Correct [with whichever words are misrecognized]**.

The correction box will come up. If what you meant to say is an option in the box, simply say **Choose <#>** and choose the corresponding number beside the correct choice. If the exact choice is not available, choose the choice closest to what you would like and say, **Edit <#>**.

Although you can technically use the **Spell That** command and use your voice to make this correction, I don't recommend it. It does not work well. After you choose the edit command, I suggest you make the correction with your keyboard. It is much more efficient. If you have mobility challenges and cannot type, you can use the **Spell That** command and use your voice. Just say the alphabet letters as you normally would. The International Radio Alphabet does not work here. Additionally, if you want your letters to be lowercase, you have to say **No Caps** first.

Unlike its Windows counterpart, you cannot train words from the correction box in Dragon® Dictate. The only way to train words is after you add them to your custom vocabulary. Don't train your words at the same time as you add them to your custom vocabulary if you are using Dragon® Dictate 6.0.8. This seems to make the program unstable and causes it to crash. Wait until your words are added and your vocabulary is saved. After that point, you can go in and click on an individual word and then click on the gear in the lower left corner and choose train. After you've done that, click 'record' and just say the word as you have chosen the spoken form to be and click 'done'.

If you are trying to correct a number or a contraction, Dragon® may pop up an additional window with smart formatting options and ask you if you want all forms of similar words to have the same form. For example, if you correct 100% so it reads one hundred percent, Dragon® will bring up a smart formatting box which will ask you how you want Dragon® to treat future instances of the word. If you want Dragon® to do nothing, you can just close the box. Otherwise, choose your favorite option among the choices presented.

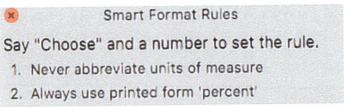

Example of Smart Formatting Dialog Box

Some users have reported an increase in their accuracy rates after correcting several documents. Many others, like myself, report no appreciable change. If you're having difficulties with your accuracy rate, it may be worth trying to see if it helps you. However, don't be discouraged if you correct a few documents and don't see a lot of change. It's one of the shortcomings of Dragon® Dictate and it doesn't reflect on your abilities at all. Even so, many authors, like myself, prefer using Dragon® Dictate because of the applications available on the Mac side of things. Now that you're set up and you know how to correct your mistakes, we can talk about what works with your Dragon® Dictate for Mac.

Using Dragon® Dictate with Other Applications

Dragon® Dictate is definitely one of those mixed blessings. It's easy to install and set up, but it's glitchy and tends to crash unexpectedly. That's the primary reason I tell people to never *ever* use Dragon® Pad. Dragon® Pad is Dragon® Dictate's built-in program for dictation when an app does not support direct dictation. Unfortunately, Dragon® Pad is prone to crashing all on its own. If it has a meltdown when you are using it, everything you've dictated will disappear when it crashes.

Save yourself the despair and don't use it. Seriously.

There are lots of other options, many of them are built right into your Mac. First, I frequently dictate right into Notes. It has a very small footprint on your computer in terms of resource allocation and it is automatically backed up. TextEdit works well too —although I find it's difficult to focus on for long periods of time.

I don't work with Pages very often, but it does not seem to present the same problems with lag which are present with Microsoft Word. Dragon® Dictate does have full editing capabilities in Pages, so you can edit and correct your errors.

I dictate into Grammarly a lot. Before Scrivener upgraded to Scrivener 3, I used to dictate into Grammarly first and then copy my work into Scrivener. Since the upgrade to Scrivener 3, I no longer do this, but I still use Grammarly when I dictate business correspondence, entries on my website or posts for social media.

Every author I know has their favorite writing tools. Mine happens to be Scrivener. It was the reason I made the switch to the Mac platform over four years ago. Before then, I had never even touched a Macintosh machine. I was a diehard Windows fan and had only used Dragon® NaturallySpeaking. However, Scrivener changed the way I write, and after hanging out on the Scrivener forum, it became clear that the Mac version of the program had more robust features than the Windows version.

I was incredibly frustrated with the whole process of copying and pasting my work into the Windows version of Scrivener. So, I made the leap across platforms to the Mac. I like dictating directly into Scrivener and Dragon® Dictate 6.0.8 works beautifully with Scrivener 3. In earlier versions, occasionally Dragon® would get lost and jump around. Scrivener 3 doesn't seem susceptible to that glitch. I love being able to organize my work, compiling it any way I please and saving it in multiple formats.

Use noise-canceling headphones to block out the sound of your voice. You will be less critical of your own mistakes.

Whatever tool you choose to use with Dragon® Dictate, it will function better if it has more resources to work with. Make sure you are running as few programs as possible while you are dictating.

Whenever possible, divide dictation sessions into smaller sections. Dragon® keeps the history of your document in a cache to aid in correction and editing later. By keeping each individual document small, you can keep the drain on resources manageable. When I write in Scrivener, I write each scene separately. If a chapter goes much beyond two thousand words without a natural scene break, I will often dictate it in different files and manually put them together at the end of the chapter just to facilitate smooth dictation.

If you find that your dictation with Dragon Dictate is lagging behind, you might try updating your operating system to Mojave (Apple's latest operating system 10.14). I have found it to be appreciably faster than High Sierra, with all other things being equal. So, if your computer is eligible for the upgrade, it is definitely worth trying.

Now that you've chosen which is voice recognition product is right for you, it is time to integrate the software into your writing routine. For some folks, this is a painless process. For others, it takes a little getting used to. Don't worry, the next chapter has lots of tips to get you started.

Chapter 6

Transitioning from Keyboard to Voice

How Do I Speak My Thoughts?

Okay, you've got it all installed, set up and ready to go, now what? For a lot of people, this is where the panic sets in. How do I speak my books out loud? Even for me, making the transition to writing creatively with voice activation software was odd. It's one thing to dictate a straightforward business memo, it's another thing to combine dictation with your creative thought process. It is a unique skill. It takes practice to build.

If you're new to dictation, one of the biggest barriers can be getting used to hearing yourself talk. From a young age, many of us get nervous performing in front of other people, and in some ways, dictation feels like a performance. If you remember that dictation is simply another means of putting information into your computer, you'll feel less pressure. After all, when was the last time you judged someone based on their keyboarding skills?

If you are uncomfortable listening to the sound of your own voice, I urge you to take time to practice dictating in an environment where the stakes don't matter. At this point, it doesn't really matter what you dictate. You can read from the newspaper, a magazine or your favorite book. You can dictate letters to your friends and family or plan what you would do if you won the lottery.

I recommend using noise-canceling headphones. My personal favorites at the moment are the Solo Beats 3. They are wireless and have exceptional battery life. This is important to me because my cell phone no longer has a headphone jack.

My cell phone plays an integral role in my writing. I stream music all day, every day, as I dictate. Basic mellow country music does it for me. I choose music where I don't think about lyrics too much. I know the songs well enough that the music fades in the background. I once tried the fancy white noise companies like Brain FM and I struggled. My brain was working too hard to try to make sense of the sound rather than focusing on the task I was supposed to be doing. I play my music through my cell phone, so it does not interfere with the operation of my computer and further stress my laptop's resources.

There is no right way to approach dictation. Some people prefer no music when they dictate, while other people prefer music with no lyrics or nonsensical white noise. If you're not sure, just play around and see what works for you.

If you're really nervous about speaking your words out loud or you dictate not so family-friendly-material, there is an option that is becoming more common in dictation circles. It is a privacy mask typically used by court reporters and it is sold by Talk Tech. I'll include a link in the Resource Guide, in case you're interested.

The second tip is to acknowledge that you will make mistakes. Whenever we have to verbalize things, there's room for error. All you have to do is look on the Internet for flubs from reporters to know this is the case. It's no different when you're dictating. You'll trip over your tongue, or you'll intend to say something, but your brain will have a different idea. You don't have to be perfect right out of the gate. **Scratch That** may very well be your favorite command in the beginning. Even thirty years in, some days I feel like I delete more than I write.

In the beginning I often advise people to cover their monitor, so they don't get focused on correcting every single mistake as they make it. There is a certain ebb and flow to dictation. As I explained before, Dragon® does better when it has more words to work with. It determines which word to use through context. If you're dictating one or two words at a time, your error rate will go up simply because the program doesn't have enough context to make the right word choices.

I can hear the panic now. A lot of authors have the misconception that they have to have a fully developed outline in order to dictate. I know this is not true. In the writing world, I am known as a pantser. Politely put, this means I write by the seat of my pants. Personally, I start out with an idea, character names and a blank page. It is quite possible I might write faster if I had an outline. However, I'm almost certain the process of trying to write an outline and sticking to it would drive me crazy. So, just take my word for it: you do not have to have a fully formed outline to be able to dictate.

Covering your monitor is a scary thought for a lot of people. You may wonder how you'll know if you make mistakes? You won't. That's the point. The idea of the exercise is to not monitor how well you're doing while you're talking. The idea is just to talk.

But, wait… What about punctuation and fixing my mistakes?

For now, we are going to table the idea of fixing mistakes. Don't worry, we'll come back to that.

As for punctuation, you need to learn to do that right away. I know, it seems daunting — but it's really not. Sooner than you think, you'll be dictating punctuation in your voicemails (and other random places). It will become so second nature, you won't think about it.

Although there are hundreds of commands available, there are only about fifteen commands in Dragon®, I use on a regular basis.

Commonly Used Commands

Command	Result
Period	.
Question Mark	?
Exclamation Mark	!
Comma	,
Open Quote	"
Close Quote	"
Colon	:
Semi Colon	;
Open Paren	(
Close Paren	)
em-dash	—
New Line	Moves to the next line.
Go to End	Moves the cursor to the end of the document.
Scatch That	Deletes the last thing you dictated.
Correct That	Corrects the last thing you dictated.

Commonly Used Commands

As you become familiar with dictation, you may add more punctuation marks and commands to your vocabulary. But, these will get you started. Whenever you get stuck, you can always say, **What Can I Say**. This brings up a contextual help menu. If you click on commands, it will give you a list of commands. If you click on the help button, it will bring up a website and you can search for whatever topic you wish — like punctuation.

It might feel a little foreign to dictate punctuation at first; it takes practice. If you have material you have already written available, practice with your own writing. At first, dictating punctuation may feel clumsy. It is tempting to just skip this step and go back and edit in your punctuation later, but I promise you it will be much quicker to learn to dictate your punctuation right from the start. You will soon get into the rhythm of dictating your commas, periods and quotation marks.

During this step, don't worry too much about correcting your mistakes. The goal here is to just get accustomed to the mechanics of speaking punctuation out loud. It is also a good time to get used to the rhythm and cadence of speaking into your microphone for dictation purposes. To the extent that you can, you want an even pace. Believe it or not, slowing down or speaking in a monotone does not help voice recognition software perform more effectively, and it adds additional stress to your vocal cords. As you get more practiced with dictation, you can speak a little faster than your normal speaking pace.

There are some other commands which are helpful to know. They deal with navigating around your document. Once again, the commands are slightly different in Dragon® NaturallySpeaking and Dragon® Dictate. As always, you can say **What Can I Say?** anytime you need assistance, but I have compiled a chart with the most common commands to get you started.

Helpful Commands for Navigating

	Dragon NaturallySpeaking	Dragon Dictate
Move to the top	Go to Top	Go to Beginning
Move to the bottom	Go to Bottom	Go to End
Move the cursor to the end of the line	Go to End of Line	
Move the cursor to the beginning of the line	Go to Beginning of Line	
Move back or forward [X] # of words	Move left/right <n> words	Move forward/backward [number] words
Move the insertion point before or after a word	Insert before/after [text]	Insert before/after [text]
Move to next line	New Line	New Line
Add a blank line	New Paragraph	New Paragraph

Helpful Commands for Navigating

Tips and Tricks

Creative writing of any sort is a skill. There is some debate about whether it is an intrinsic talent you are born with or whether it can be learned. Either way, it is something you get better at as you practice. It is like running. You can't wake up one day and decide to be an elite marathon runner. It's something you have to work your way up to.

I don't recommend switching to voice recognition software when you're facing down a huge deadline. Although the additional output might be helpful during your crunch time, there is no guarantee you're going to reach peak productivity right up front. Some people take to dictation like they were born to do it. To those people — kudos! Go forth and populate the world with your words. Other people struggle a little with the transition.

Even I had a bit of difficulty when I entered the world of creative writing. When I first started tracking my numbers, writing five hundred words a day seemed like a big challenge. I was caught up in the pursuit of perfection at the cost of getting words down on paper. These days, when I'm writing fiction, a three thousand-word day is a little more typical, and I have written as many as eighteen thousand words in one day. I don't recommend too many days like that, because they can be hard on your voice, but it was a fun challenge.

Before you get started using dictation on a regular basis, it's important to remember you need to take care of your voice just like you take care of your fingers and wrists and shoulders when you type. Your voice can become fatigued. You can get a sore throat and lose your voice from overuse.

My first word of caution: don't get dehydrated. You'll be surprised by how much you need to drink when you talk constantly. I know coffee is the unofficial beverage of choice for exhausted authors everywhere — but it is good to drink water as well. Coffee can actually be dehydrating. Milk-based drinks are not particularly good for your voice because they encourage the production of mucus which is hard on your vocal cords.

When I'm participating in one of my marathon sessions, I like to drink warm tea with lemon and honey as well.

Speaking of honey, I swear by honey cough drops by Burt's Bees.

I try not to dictate for more than fifty minutes at a time without taking a break. If I'm sprinting, I don't do more than three fifty minute sessions without taking an extended break.

As I mentioned before, I didn't start out being able to dictate for such long periods of time. This was something I worked my way up to. In the beginning, you may only have the endurance to do a few minutes at a time. If you grow hoarse, you need to take a break. That's a sign of stress on your vocal cords. Long-term, chronic overuse can do permanent damage.

At the risk of sounding like the mother I am, good posture and breath support will help your dictation. Also, keeping the microphone close enough to your mouth that you don't need to project your voice will reduce vocal fatigue.

If you live in a dry environment, a humidifier can reduce the strain on your voice.

Ideally, if you're sick, try not to dictate. However, I know that's not always realistic. As you may have noticed, I actually have a profile named Mary with a cold. I have asthma and I often have upper respiratory infections. If I had to cease dictating every time I felt under the weather, I wouldn't get much done. If you're like me and you fight chronic illness, sometimes you just have to work around it. On the days you don't feel well, try to shorten your dictation sessions and take frequent breaks. If you have to take decongestants, remember to increase your fluid intake to compensate.

We've talked about ways to protect your voice and the importance of dictating your punctuation. Now it's time to get started.

When I first started writing fiction, I didn't realize it would be different from dictating business memos or reports. I quickly learned writing creatively and dictating at the same time takes a different set of skills than I was used to in the business world. I was also amazed to hear other authors say that if an author dictated their words, they weren't really writing. The first time I heard the criticism, I thought for sure I misheard the speaker. Then I read the same criticism online where there was no mistaking the intent. Trust me, I work just as hard to speak my words as the person who writes them by hand or types them on a keyboard. They are just as real; there is nothing less authentic about my words. Dictation is merely another input device — it's not a "cheat". If you encounter similar pushback, disregard it.

When you first start using dictation, the temptation is to dictate task lists. You can do that. In fact, I often dictate my grocery list. However, it won't really help you develop the skill to dictate and think creatively at the same time.

I often challenge authors to think outside the box for a bit if they are finding it difficult to come up with ideas to dictate about. Put away your plots and outlines and think fancifully a minute.

Here are some prompts you can use. If you don't like mine, there are many prompt generators available online. I particularly like the ones available at NaNoWriMo.org.

What would you do if you won the lottery? What if you could only keep half of the money and you had to spend the rest anonymously, but you had to choose a group of junior high school students to spend it? How would you give them instructions?

If you could go back and give yourself advice when you were a freshman in high school, what would you tell yourself? What would you tell your teachers? What would you tell your parents?

If you could reinvent one piece of technology, what would it be? How would it function differently?

The idea of these prompts is not to have a fully structured story idea, or a perfectly formed outline. It is just to get you to think creatively. In order to get the full benefit of this exercise, you need to use proper sentence structure and punctuation, including quotation marks, commas and periods.

Try to use a mixture of punctuation. Dictate dialogue with some question marks and exclamation points. If you write nonfiction and bullets are your thing, try to add bullets and indents to your dictation to see how it feels. (The command for adding bullets in Dragon® Dictate is **Bullet That**. For Dragon® NaturallySpeaking, the command is **Make That Bullet Style**.)

Remember the correction tool in Dragon® is intended for misrecognized words, not to edit for clarity.

After you have completed a writing exercise, (a thousand or so words will work just fine), if you are using Dragon® NaturallySpeaking, you need to go back and correct any recognition mistakes. Dragon® seems to learn more efficiently if you correct your mistakes by voice, but using your keyboard is better than not correcting mistakes at all. Remember, you can always ask Dragon® NaturallySpeaking to playback what you said if you don't remember.

If you are using Dragon® Dictate, you can skip this step if you choose, because the improvement you will receive through correcting your mistakes is negligible. The **Play That Back** command in Dragon® Dictate uses whatever automated voice you have set up in your preferences.

The writing you do during these exercises doesn't have to be grammatically perfect or follow any rigid structure. The idea behind them is to get you used to a new form of input. You might be tempted to simply trash these writing exercises. You can if you wish, but I recommend you save them in a file somewhere. It is fun to go back and see where you started.

All this might be interesting and fun, but where does the speed come in? Don't worry, I'm getting there. I just want you to be comfortable with the process of writing creatively without a keyboard before you try to do it quickly. After you've done a few exercises and you are comfortable combining dictation with writing creatively, the fastest way I know to increase your writing speed is to introduce timed sprints.

Sprinting

If you've been around the writing community for very long, you've probably heard of the concept of sprints or word wars. Like everything else when it comes to writing, no single approach works for everyone. Sprinting seems to be especially controversial. People either love it or hate it. You certainly don't have to sprint to be successful at dictation. However, successful sprinting and dictation share many of the same building blocks.

Sprinting is just a fancy name for timed writing. You write as many words in a particular time period as you can manage. Sprinting is an effective method for getting lots of words on the page because it forces you to turn off your inner editor and simply write. To be effective at writing, you can't write and edit at the same time. Doing both can stifle your creativity. Writing under time pressure forces you to choose writing over editing. This same time pressure will often encourage you to speak in longer strings of words, which is better for accurate dictation.

When you first start sprinting, I recommend starting with short sprints. I always start with an initial ten-minute sprint. This allows me to ease into my day of sprinting. Usually, my first sprint of the day is a little choppy and not very fluid. It's almost as if I have to wake up my voice and sync it with my brain.

If you are new to sprinting and dictation, you might want to stick with fifteen-minute sprinting sessions for a while. Many writers I know stick to fifteen or twenty-minute sprinting sessions and never increase their time limits. They find shorter sessions are great for their productivity. If that strategy works for you, great!

Personally, I prefer fifty-minute sprints. It usually takes me a while to get into the rhythm of dictating. When I participate in short sprints with my friends, I often feel like I just got started when the sprint is over. The important thing is to find a length that works well for you.

Speaking of timing, you'll need to find a convenient way to time your sprints. I like to use an app called Tomato One. Your timer on your phone will work just fine. I know other writers who use an old-fashioned kitchen timer.

The nice thing about the Tomato One timer, as opposed to some other *Pomodoro* timers on the market, is that you can adjust the settings to your own personal preferences. Although I typically like to set my sprints for fifty minutes and take ten-minute breaks; on the days I'm feeling particularly burnt out, I back those numbers down to thirty-minute sprints and ten-minute breaks. Some days, when I'm feeling particularly scattered, I may only manage fifteen-minute sprints.

Sprints are great for keeping your writing hat on and putting the editing hat away for a while. Sprints become especially fun when you are racing against other authors. I find sprinting with groups of other authors helps me stay off of social media and on task. It's a way to be accountable and focused. I will put some of my favorite sprinting sites in the resource guide at the end of this book.

I have developed some tricks to sprint faster over the years. If you encounter something along the way, you need to research while you are sprinting, simply say **Open Square Bracket/Close Square Bracket**. For example, in this book when I was dictating about minimum RAM requirements, I didn't know them off the top of my head, so I wrote [RAM requirement] while I was sprinting and went back and researched the actual requirement later on one of my breaks. I normally write contemporary romance novels and my characters frequently are involved in activities I know nothing about. That often requires me to research on the fly. So, if I'm sprinting I will use square brackets to indicate an area in which I need to go back and research later. I choose square brackets because they are easy to find and replace when I am editing. I also use this option when I can't remember the words on the tip of my tongue. Often, I will get tired of repeating the same word, but in the rush of a sprint, my brain just doesn't want to act like a thesaurus. I just use the simple word and offset it in square brackets to remind myself I want to come back and use a more sophisticated choice later.

Of course, as with any first draft writing, when you finish your manuscript, it's not ready for publication; you'll need to edit your work. For the most part, I don't use Dragon® to edit — unless I'm inserting large blocks of text to fill a plot hole or making other substantial scene edits.

Sprinting is one tool for getting lots of words down quickly. Other authors report great success with methods like transcription which allow them to get away from the computer.

Chapter 7

Taking Things Mobile

Transcription

Transcription is another tool you can use to increase your production numbers while freeing yourself from the constraints of being tied down to your computer. Authors who have made the transition to transcription report a sharp increase in the number of words they dictate per day. There's something about the idea of unplugging from a monitor and simply letting the ideas flow that really speeds up the process. I don't use transcription often, but I can confirm that my output is higher if I transcribe than if I dictate in front of my computer.

Transcription is great for increasing your productivity as a writer because it allows you to dictate in blocks of time where you might not otherwise be able to. Stuck in the carpool lane waiting to pick up your kids after school? No problem! You can dictate lots of words in twenty minutes. Have a few minutes on your lunch hour, but don't want to use the company computer to write your steamy shifter romance? Transcription may be the answer.

Remember back in the beginning, when I suggested that you acclimate yourself to dictating by covering your monitor? That exercise was really good preparation for what you'll experience when you transcribe. It is a little disconcerting to dictate without having a monitor in front of you. It's the ultimate experience of riding a bicycle without training wheels. On the other hand, it is this detachment from the constant feedback of the monitor which gives you the freedom to dictate quickly without the compulsion to correct your mistakes.

I need to talk for a moment about what transcription is not. It is not a substitute for a court reporter or a real-time captioner. Although Dragon®

Professional Individual allows you the option to set up a profile for a speaker other than yourself, it means one other speaker — not a room full of speakers. You cannot set your recorder up in the middle of a staff meeting and expect Dragon® to reliably transcribe all the voices in the room. There are other technologies available for that type of situation. The transcription function in Dragon® is not intended to function that way.

If you are going to be transcribing files for another speaker, make sure you check the box that indicates that the speaker is not you. Otherwise, Dragon® will adapt your profile based on the transcription files of the other speaker.

Transcription is one area in which both Dragon® Dictate and Dragon® NaturallySpeaking have radically improved over the years. The software is much easier to use than it used to be. Again, you need a quality microphone and a relatively quiet environment for it to function at its optimal level, but if you haven't tried transcription recently, I urge you to give it a try.

Setting up transcription for Dragon® Dictate and Dragon® NaturallySpeaking differ slightly. So, I will address them separately. However, there are common elements under both, so I'll talk about them briefly here.

First, you will need something to record your transcription files. You can use your smart phone to record files or you can purchase an external recording device. Initially, I chose a digital recorder. I have an Olympus WS 853. This is a good option because it is small and compact, and it has rechargeable batteries. It allows you to go back and erase your mistakes if you choose.

However, I find it easiest just to use my cell phone. I use an app called Voice Record Pro. I chose this application because it is simple and straightforward. I can easily change the settings to mono — which is the preferred setting for transcription and choose the type of file I want saved. It also gives the opportunity for me to rename the file. This is handy when you are dictating scenes.

You may have noticed throughout this book that many of my cautionary tales have a ring of truth. There's a reason for that. Many of the lessons I've learned, I have acquired the hard way — the following story is no exception. When I first got my digital recorder, I was really excited. I dictated a long and complicated scene. I waited with bated breath to see my words magically appear on the screen. I was horrified when forty-five minutes worth of dictation yielded only about ten words which were recognizable. The rest of it was pure gibberish.

At first, I wondered if all my friends who were huge proponents of transcription were playing a giant hoax on me. Why were they able to get such phenomenal results when all I could produce was garbage? Upon further investigation, I discovered I plugged in my lapel microphone to the wrong port. After I hooked up everything properly, my output improved dramatically.

Before you attempt to dictate anything long and complex, do a couple of test recordings to make sure your equipment is operating properly, and you understand the importing and file conversion process. One of the nice features about transcription is that it can be done in the background. Dragon® needs about a minute of processing time per minute of dictation.

If Dragon® is having difficulty deciphering your audio files, you might want to check the quality of your files with a third-party application like Audacity. Listen to the files. Check to see that your speech is crisp and clear and there isn't an overabundance of background noise. If there is, you might need to adjust the position of your microphone or use a higher-quality notice-canceling mic. Several people I know who are avid fans of transcription — especially those who like to transcribe while they are doing outdoor activities like walking, swear by the FlexyMic.

One of the big concerns with transcription is what to do if you make a mistake. After all, you can't exactly stop and start over. (Well, I guess you could, but it wouldn't be very productive.) When I first started transcribing, this caused me a great deal of anxiety. After all, I had years of — admittedly bad — habits to break. But I have developed a strategy if I make a mistake. It's my own code. When I make a mistake, I say *Nullify That*. If I know the exact number of sentences, I will say *Nullify Last Two Sentences* or *Nullify Last Block of Dialogue*. I will then re-dictate it. When I am done, I will say *Proceed From Here*.

After I have transcribed my document into an RTF file, I copy and paste it into my Scrivener file and do a search function for the words *nullify* and *proceed from*. Because they are unusual words, it makes it really easy to go back and clean up any mistakes I made while dictating.

The knowledge that I did not have to accept the mistakes I made in my document was key to helping me become comfortable with transcription. Knowing this made we able to relax and enjoy the creative process without worrying if I would make a mistake while I dictated. I hope this little trick allows you to explore the world of transcription and see if it works for you.

First, I'll talk about using transcription with Dragon® Professional Individual 15.3 for Windows and then I will have a section on using it with Dragon® Professional Individual 6.0.8 for Mac.

In many places in this book, my advice is applicable regardless of which version of NaturallySpeaking you are currently using. This is not the case with transcription. Nuance® has made some substantial changes to its user interface with Dragon® Professional Individual 15.3, so the instructions I give here are specific to version 15.3.

Nuance® has streamlined the process a great deal. You do not have to create a new profile or specify a new dictation source specific to transcription unless you are not the speaker whose words are being transcribed. However, whenever you make big changes to your profile, you should save your profile and a copy of your custom vocabulary words to an external drive in case you ever have to restore it for any reason.

Again, unless you're going to be transcribing someone else's voice, you don't have to set up a special profile for transcription. But if you are going to be transcribing someone else's voice, this is how you set up a profile.

After you plug in your microphone (this step won't work without one) click on 'Profile' located on the Dragon® Bar then click 'New User Profile'. Click 'New', and then click Next.

Transcription Setup for Dragon Professional Individual 15.3

Choose a name for your profile. I like to include the word transcription in the profile name, so I know it has a distinct purpose. Make sure you check the box which indicates you are setting this profile up for another speaker's transcription. This is critically important this is what tells Dragon® not to save any of the data related to transcription done under this profile to your speech files.

Next, set up is just like when you set up a regular profile — you'll choose an accent and a region for the speaker you'll be transcribing. Dragon® will also ask you if you want to help them collect anonymous data to improve their files. After you have chosen that option, your set up will be finished and you can use your file for transcription. Note: When you are in transcription mode, the microphone will be grayed out with an X through it.

If you have transcribed under previous versions of Dragon® NaturallySpeaking, things have changed. You no longer need a dedicated transcription source or profile. You only need an audio file in a format Dragon® NaturallySpeaking can read. Acceptable format types include: .wav, .mp3, .wma, .dss, .ds2, and .m4a. Most digital recorders will allow you to choose the format in which you save your file. If yours does not, the iTunes app and Windows Media Player will both allow you to convert audio files.

To change to Transcription Mode in Dragon® NaturallySpeaking, go to the Tools menu on the Dragon® Bar and choose 'Transcribe Audio' and then choose 'Transcribe Recording'. Alternatively, you can say **Transcribe Recording**.

Doing either of those things will bring up the following box:

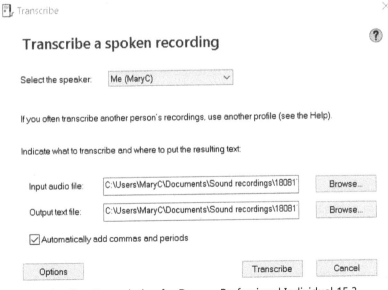

Uploading Transcription for Dragon Professional Individual 15.3

In the top box, you will select the speaker. Unless you have set up a separate transcription profile to transcribe files for another speaker, this will just be your regular dictation profile. In the next box, you will pick where your audio file is located. In the box below that, you will pick where you would like your output file to be saved. If you do not have a separate file set up, it will default to the same file where your audio file was located. You can check the box to automatically add commas and periods. I do not check this box because after thirty years of dictation, I am conditioned to automatically dictate punctuation on my own — but you can use this option if you wish.

There is a button for advanced options. You can choose what level of commands you want to be recognized while you transcribe. You can choose to have Dragon® ignore most commands. This can be a handy feature if you tend to stop and start a lot when you dictate into a recorder and you are afraid the program might interpret the pause as a command. When you are done choosing your options, simply choose 'Transcribe'.

Now the transcribing begins. It can take some time for the program to complete its work. Be patient. This process can be done in the background, so you can do other things. When the transcription is complete, you will be given the option to open the results in Dragon® Pad, Microsoft Word or copy transcription to the clipboard.

Per my usual recommendation, I suggest you choose Microsoft Word as the landing zone for your transcription file if that is an option for you. Like many other long-term users of Dragon® products, I've been burned by Dragon® Pad a few too many times to trust it.

Look over the transcription results for any misrecognized words. If you find any, you can correct them as you would any other mistake Dragon® makes. This improves your overall accuracy as well as how well Dragon® interprets your audio files. When you are finished correcting your file, you can just copy and paste it into whatever word-processing file you are comfortable using.

Dragon® NaturallySpeaking automatically shifts back to dictation mode after your file has been processed. However, if you are ever stuck in transcription mode after you've worked with a different transcribing profile, just click on Profile and open your regular profile.

I'll be the first to admit I don't use transcription as much as I should. Dragon® Professional Individual 6.0.8 has taken away the last of my excuses. I can no longer claim it's too difficult or cumbersome for me to use.

To start the process of transcribing in Dragon® dictate, all you have to say is **Transcription Mode,** or you can just click on the Dragon® symbol in the menu bar and 'Switch to Transcription'. A window will pop up giving you the option to choose your user, the type of file you want to save the output as, and an opportunity to upload the audio file.

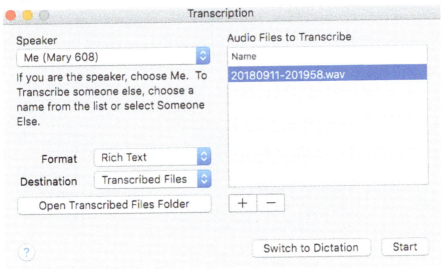

Choosing File for Transcription For Dragon Professional Individual 6.0.8

If you click on someone else as an option under speaker, it will give you the option to create a profile. It will ask you to choose a region and an accent similar to the way it does when you set up a profile for dictating. The name you chose will now appear on the speaker list.

You can save the format as an RTF file or a Microsoft Word document and you can choose a custom location for your files. Then you press the plus button to add your files. You may have more than one. When you're finished, you press the start button.

After your file is finished processing, Dragon® Pad will open or your file will appear in Microsoft Word.

Contrary to popular belief, you can improve the accuracy of your transcription through training in Dragon® Professional Individual 6.0.8. The process just looks different in Dragon® Dictate than it does a Dragon® NaturallySpeaking. To begin the training process, click on the Dragon® symbol in the menu bar.

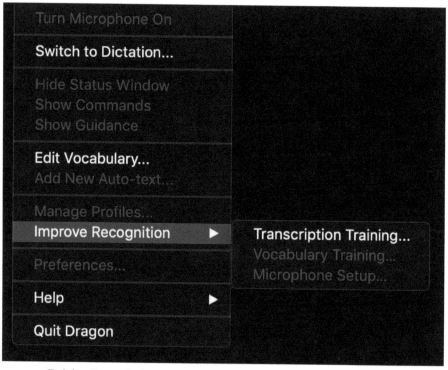

Training Transcription Menu For Dragon Professional Individual 6.0.8

You'll be asked to upload an audio file. Be aware this file needs to be several minutes long in order for Dragon® to complete its process. It will warn you if you do not have a sufficiently large sample size.

The program will process your audio file and place it into a window like the one below. You will then have a chance to accept or ignore the selections. You can fix an incorrect interpretation of your speech with your keyboard. Throughout the process, you can listen to any of the samples to make sure you hear what Dragon® heard.

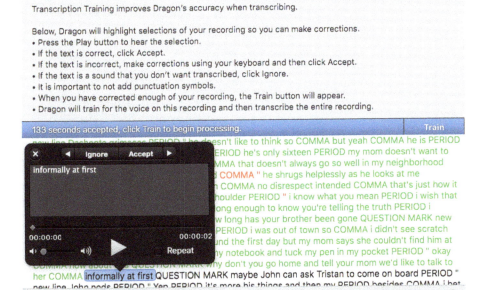

Training Transcription Files For Dragon Professional individual 6.0.8

After you have corrected enough of the sample, the Train button will appear and Dragon® Dictate will reprocess your transcription with the corrections.

It is important to note that although it looks like there are no capital letters after the periods in the training material, in the actual transcription, all the sentences are capitalized appropriately. For the most part, I found most of the errors in the transcription occurred because my speech was not clear. In the above example, it made an error on the word sixty and sixteen — but to be honest, it was difficult to determine which word I actually said.

Unlike its Windows counterpart, you cannot choose to have Dragon® Dictate automatically insert periods and commas.

When you are done training your transcription for accuracy, you will need to switch back to dictation mode. Unfortunately, you can't do this by voice. You'll have to go up to the Dragon® symbol and click on 'Switch to Dictation'

Dragon® Anywhere

Several authors I know love to write on their tablets and phones with Bluetooth keyboards. Nuance®'s solution to this is Dragon® Anywhere. Tablets and phones come with built-in voice activation programs such as Siri or Google. However, even though the speech-to-text capability is handy, it is severely limiting because it only allows you to dictate in very short bursts of text and the correction and punctuation features are quite limited.

Recent updates to Dragon® Anywhere have improved its interface a great deal. It now functions much more like the regular desktop versions of Dragon® NaturallySpeaking or Dragon® Dictate. Corrections are much easier and navigating around the screen is much more intuitive. With Dragon® Anywhere, you can now automatically back up your work to Dropbox and Evernote. Unfortunately, it does not yet automatically sync with mobile versions of Microsoft Word or Scrivener. I hope those upgrades are coming soon. It is a very expensive piece of software at fifteen dollars a month to lack such basic compatibility.

Interestingly enough, on my MacBook Pro, the internal mic is astonishingly accurate. The internal mic on my iPhone 7 also did an admirable job. It was more accurate than my wireless headphones. Accuracy is important with this product because corrections are difficult.

Dragon® Anywhere is not the product for you if you have to work hands-free. If you make an error and Dragon® does not recognize the word you said, and the proper answer is not in the correction box, you cannot correct the mistake with your voice; you must repeat the word until Dragon® guesses the right choice or correct it with your keyboard. As you might guess, this approach is less than ideal for productivity.

Custom vocabulary words are a valuable tool when you're working with complex character names.

One feature that carries over from Dragon® NaturallySpeaking, which I enjoy, is the ability to select a range of text by selecting the first word of the text through the last word. In addition to automatically backing up your dictation to Dropbox and Evernote, you can also use traditional copy and paste techniques to transfer your dictation to different applications like Scrivener or Microsoft Word.

Additionally, if you're using unique character names or industry specific terms, you do have the option to add them to your vocabulary and make them custom words. As I've mentioned before, my favorite feature of Dragon® Anywhere is its ability to sync your custom vocabulary words across all of your platforms if you have other versions of Dragon® Professional Individual. Honestly, this is the primary reason I continue to pay the monthly fee. Absent this feature, I don't use it enough to justify the cost.

Although I hesitate to recommend Dragon® Anywhere as someone's primary dictation tool, if you like to dictate using your phone or a tablet, you might find Dragon® Anywhere useful.

Chapter 8

Increasing your Productivity

Using Custom Words and Phrases

There are several ways you can use the programming features within Dragon® to increase your productivity. These include the use of custom vocabulary words, custom commands, and managing your profiles.

I touched a little on using custom vocabulary words a bit earlier, but I really think it's one of the most powerful tools we have within dictation. Right out of the box, both Dragon® Dictate and Dragon® NaturallySpeaking are remarkably accurate when they are set up properly with a good quality microphone on an appropriate computer, in a suitable environment. In fact, when I tried to induce mistakes, so I would have examples to correct for demonstration purposes, it was remarkably difficult.

Having said that, custom vocabulary words are invaluable when you're working with character names. I have a couple of strategies I use when working with difficult names. First, if I want to dictate in a hurry, I'll use simple names which don't have multiple spellings, like Sally and Travis, and when the novel is done, I go back and replace them using find and replace for the actual names I intended to use all along.

However, sometimes my brain just doesn't cooperate with the easy way of doing things and I have to do it the hard way. In one of my novels, I have Native American characters named Tayanita and Ketki. So, when I added their names to the custom vocabulary list, I added spoken forms of their names. In addition, I ran several documents through the Vocabulary Trainer with their names used in dialogue and in sentences.

Another of my books has a character named Darya. For some reason, if I put Darya in the custom vocabulary list as just Darya (even after I added and trained the spoken form), Dragon® always interprets it as Darius. In that case, I had to get creative and amend the spoken form to say, "character Darya". In another instance, I have a different character named Kennadie. However, no matter how hard I tried, the spelling was always wrong. So, I added a spoken form and called her "baby Kennedy".

It is quite simple to set up a custom vocabulary word. Simply go to the menu and choose edit vocabulary. Choose the + and click on it. You can add your word with your keyboard or your voice. If you want a spoken explanation for your word, you can add it here. I will often add a spoken variation if my custom word is readily mistaken for another word. For example, I have a character named Maddie. Dragon® was always confusing her for Mattie. To compensate for this, I added Mattie as the spoken variation of Maddie.

There are also options to make custom commands. The easiest of these are Auto Texts. You can use auto texts to generate longer chunks of texts such as your signature, your address, email address or the standard closing of a letter. Auto texts are really easy to set up. You just need to choose a unique name and then add your text below.

If you are interested in adding more complex commands, Nuance® has videos and handbooks available on their website. As I said, I am not a computer programmer and I don't know how to write script. Knowbrainer. com has some information on their website about writing complex script and making commands as well.

Multiple Profiles

Most people can completely disregard the advice I'm going to talk about now. It simply isn't required by the vast majority of authors. However, I wanted to touch on assigning specialized vocabularies to multiple profiles for the small number of authors who may be affected.

For authors who write in dramatically different genres, Dragon® NaturallySpeaking has the ability to add unique custom vocabularies to different profiles. In most cases, this is unnecessary. However, if you think Dragon® will confuse your character names or, if for one genre you've taught Dragon® to cuss incessantly and your other genre is squeaky clean, you might want to consider building two distinctly different profiles with different custom vocabulary lists.

Make sure you always set up a profile for the default microphone on your laptop even if you never intend to use it. This will allow you to get into your voice recognition program even if your favorite microphone malfunctions.

Remember to save each profile after you have added your custom vocabulary words and run the Vocabulary Training. I recommend saving it on an external thumb drive in case your profile somehow gets corrupted.

It is possible to have different profiles with different vocabularies under Dragon® Dictate 6.0.8. However, it is a much more arduous process. You need to back up each vocabulary on your computer and manually import the vocabularies each time you want to change it. Additionally, after you finish working with a specific vocabulary, you would have to remember to re-export it and save it before importing a different list of custom vocabulary words. You will have to weigh whether the benefit outweighs the hassle of this approach for you. For most people, I would venture to guess it is probably not.

Chapter 9

Troubleshooting Common Problems

Microphone Woes

There is nothing more discouraging than trying to get started with dictation and discovering that your microphone doesn't work. Never fear, I'll give you some tips to try to work through some common issues with your microphone.

First, make sure you always set up a profile for the default microphone on your laptop even if you never intend to use it. This will allow you to get into your voice recognition program even if your favorite microphone is not working properly. Just be sure not to set the internal microphone as your default microphone in your computer's operating system. Make your favorite USB microphone your default microphone.

Secondly, if you are using a Mac, make sure the internal microphone input is turned all the way down. Otherwise, it competes with the microphone you intend to use.

If using a Mac, make sure the internal microphone input is turned all the way down. Otherwise, it competes with the microphone you intend to use.

If I have microphone problems, the most common culprit is the USB cord. Make sure it is plugged in tightly and it hasn't developed a kink. Much like your phone charger, the wires can wear out at the places where it connects to your microphone and to your computer. Fortunately, USB cords are relatively inexpensive and can be replaced easily. My microphone is on a boom arm that gets moved frequently, so my cord is under a lot of stress. Consequently, I replace my USB cord often.

If your microphone has adjustable gain, make sure the gain setting didn't get inadvertently moved — either on the microphone itself or within your software settings.

On a related note, last year my accuracy suddenly declined. When I ran the microphone set up, I noticed upon playback my speech sounded like I was one of the long-lost members of Alvin and the Chipmunks. For some reason, the bit rate of my microphone had been changed. (It should be 44,100 Hz.) I never isolated the cause — but deleting my profile and creating a new one resolved the issue.

There is a known compatibility issue between Windows 10 and USB microphones. You may have to boost the output of your USB microphone. As of the writing of this book in the summer of 2018, this has not been resolved. However, there is a workaround within the Control Panel.

The easiest way to access this is to create a shortcut to your Control Panel. To do this, go to your Windows desktop. Right click, then select 'New', followed by 'Shortcut'.

It will ask you what you'd like the shortcut to lead to. Type in 'control.exe'.

When it asks you to name the shortcut, type in 'Control Panel'. This will give you a shortcut to the old-style Windows Control panel. It has more options than the Windows 10 control panel.

You may want to double-click it and change the options at the top to large icons so it's easier to navigate. Then look for the sound option.

Click the tab at the top of the window which reads 'Recording' and double-click your USB Microphone. Then click 'levels'. You should see a window like the one the pictured below. The bottom item is the boost setting. This allows you to boost the microphone level.

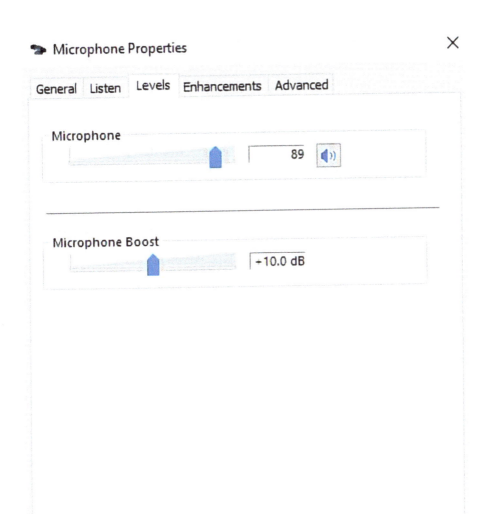

Boosting Microphone Sound In Windows

I've discovered one more issue while setting up microphones in Windows. If you have a microphone which has a jack for listening with a set of headphones, make sure the headphones you use to listen don't also have an internal mic attached. (I see your eye-roll, and in retrospect I probably deserve it — but in my defense, two other tech support people didn't figure it out either. So, just in case you are as clueless as I was, there's a little heads up for you.)

The next issue isn't really a microphone issue at all, but it can present as if there is a problem with your microphone. Dragon® products operate in distinct modes. If you do not have your product in the proper mode, it can act like your microphone is not working or it can produce gibberish when you expect it to produce words. The result can make you think your microphone is malfunctioning.

The mode most people feel comfortable in is Dictation and Command. This allows Dragon® the flexibility to recognize either dictation or commands. In order to dictate a command, you merely need to pause for the briefest second before issuing a command like **Caps On** or **Italicize That**. You can adjust the amount of time you need to pause under options in Dragon® NaturallySpeaking. If Dragon® is trying to interpret too much of your normal dictation as commands, you might want to adjust this setting.

In Dictation mode, Dragon® listens only to dictation and completely ignores most commands you would use for editing. You can still do basic commands like making capital letters or creating new lines however more complex commands are not available. However, the upside is that if your computer is light on memory, this dictation mode tends to speed up your computer and reduce lag time.

The Numbers Mode has similar restrictions. It's very handy if you are putting numbers in an Excel spreadsheet. Spelling Mode is very helpful if you're inputting serial numbers. It does respond to both traditional names for letters and the International Radio Alphabet.

If your computer is behaving erratically, make sure you're in the right mode for how you would like to dictate.

Issues Specific to Dragon® Dictate

You have a Mac. Congratulations! Dragon® Dictate 6.0.8 is all loaded, prepped and ready to go on your computer. Wonderful!

Brace yourself — your Dragon® **will** crash.

It's not the end of the world.

Dragon® Dictate will also leave behind what I affectionately call Dragon poop. Dragon poop most often consists of letters, but sometimes numbers or random punctuation left behind after it's lost its place in your document.

Don't panic!

I'll deal with the Dragon poop issue first. Because of the way the way Apple writes its code, Dragon® has a problem keeping track of where it is in your document. This is often exacerbated if you use your keyboard to input information while you are dictating. Dragon® keeps a cache of information about your document in its history to assist with editing. If you input information via your keyboard or mouse, it disrupts this record-keeping and can make the program lose its place. I recommend you refrain from touching your keyboard or mouse while you are dictating. I know this is very difficult. I struggle with this too. I've taken to wearing sweatshirts with a large pocket in the front where I place my hands while I dictate to dissuade me from using my keyboard. It's a subtle reminder to not type while I am in the process of dictating.

If Dragon® misrecognizes a command, it can cause the same problems. Try to enunciate your commands quite clearly, especially commands which end in the word 'that'.

If this happens and you see your cursor racing up the screen, simply wait for it to stop. If you see it delete a word, you can press **COMMAND + Z** to restore the deleted text. Additionally, the program may leave behind some random letters, numbers or punctuation when you try to dictate your next few words. (It is this unfortunate side effect I refer to as Dragon poop.) If this happens, simply backspace and delete those characters. The next step is to say **Cache Document**. This will empty out the cache and reset it. It will eliminate the extra characters which are appearing after your sentences.

If you have difficulty with Dragon® Dictate crashing often, first make sure you have the most recent version. At the time of the publication of this book, in summer of 2018, the most recent version of Dragon® Professional Individual for Mac is 6.0.8. The difference between Dragon® Dictate 6.0 and 6.0.8 cannot be emphasized enough. This is one piece of software you absolutely, positively need to make sure you update.

If your hard drive is stuffed to the gills, you might want to get rid of some files. Dragon® Dictate does better if it has plenty of room to operate.

Dragon® also functions better if there are very few other programs running, especially big programs like Microsoft Word or Photoshop. If I try to dictate in Microsoft Word, I keep my file size very small.

In the event Dragon® Dictate 6.0.8 has a meltdown, you are not likely to lose any information — unless you disregarded my advice and elected to use Dragon® Pad. Once again, please don't use Dragon® Pad. If you are using Dragon® Pad and Dragon® Dictate crashes, you will lose everything. My recommendation is to use a program like Grammarly, Notes or Scrivener 3, which back up automatically.

If Dragon® Dictate 6.0.8 crashes, you do not have to close down the system completely. Simply start up your Activity Monitor, which is a utility that comes standard with the Mac OS. I actually put it on my toolbar. If Dragon® Dictate becomes unresponsive, simply open the Activity Monitor.

Click on the CPU button. If Dragon® is frozen up, the application should be highlighted in red. Select it. Then click Quit and then Force Quit in the next window. This will completely close down Dragon® Dictate. You'll have to restart your application. However, this will not disturb any other applications you may have running.

Sometimes when Dragon® crashes, it will generate an error log and an automatic email to send to tech support. You can elect to attach the log and send the email to Nuance®. I'm told it helps with product development, although I have never received a response from these emails.

Over time, your profile can become degraded through ambient noise, mis-corrected words and variances in the way you use your microphone. Sometimes it's better just to start over with a fresh profile. Yet, I don't always like to choose the nuclear option of reinstalling the whole program. I do what I call a soft reset.

If you want to train your custom vocabulary words in Dragon® 6.0.8, wait until after your vocabulary words have been added and saved.

Remember back a few chapters back when I suggested you should save a copy of your profile after you've added all your custom vocabulary words and run the Vocabulary Training? This is where that comes in handy. In case you missed it — this is the easy way to save your profile.

Locating your Dragon Profile

Once you have located your profile in the Finder, make a note of both the name of the profile and the location. You will need this information later.

Choose the profile you want to backup. Copy it to a removable drive. This location is important. If you put it on your desktop or in another location on your hard drive, Dragon® can find it and it will cause a conflict within the program.

Later when you want to do a "soft reset" and restore things to the way they were when you started, close Dragon® Dictate and all other programs except Finder.

The following is an optional step, but I will often do it if I find that my profile is crashing or lagging in some way. It removes any preferences and is a factory reset of sorts.

- Open Finder.

- Go to the Go menu for Finder at the top of the screen.

- Use the Option key to choose Library.

- Go to the Preferences folder.

- Remove com.Dragon.dictate.plist by sending or dragging it to the trash.

What happens next depends on your profiles. If the profile you want to replace matches one of the profiles currently listed in your managed profiles, all you need to do is go to the location you discovered under Reveal Profile in Finder and place your obsolete profile in the trash and replace it with a copy of your fresh profile that you have saved on your external drive.

If the name is not the same, you need to take one additional step. If you've set up new profiles since you've made a backup, you need to make another profile which has the same name as your backup profile. Don't worry, it doesn't need to be anything fancy, you just need to go through the microphone setup, so the profile is created. After it is created, you can locate it in the Finder and swap it out with the profile which has your custom words and has undergone vocabulary training. Make sure you have closed Dragon® Dictate first.

Sometimes even a soft reset is not enough, and you need to uninstall Dragon® completely and start over. In Windows, you do this through the control panel, choosing the uninstall program.

On the Mac side, the uninstall process is much more involved. I've included the instructions below, but keep in mind, this is what I consider to be the nuclear option. This removes Dragon® Dictate from your system completely. To reinstall, you will have to start over again as if you never had Dragon® Dictate on your system at all.

HOW TO UNINSTALL DRAGON® DICTATE COMPLETELY

Step 1 of 8: Quit all applications.

a.) Close Dragon® for Mac by clicking on the menu bar icon and click on Quit Dictate.

b.) Choose Force Quit from the Apple menu.

c.) Force Quit applications in the Force Quit Applications window except Finder. Note: When an application is closed by force quit, any unsaved changes to open documents are not saved.

Step 2: Remove /Users/username/Library/Application Support/Dictate/

a.) Choose Go to Folder from the Go menu.

b.) Enter the following text in the Go to Folder text box: ~/Library/Application Support/Dictate/ and click Go.

c.) Move the Dictate folder to the Trash.

Step 3: Remove /Users/username/Library/Application Support/Dragon/

a.) Choose Go to Folder from the Go menu.

b.) Enter the following text in the Go to Folder text box: ~/Library/Application Support/Dragon/ and click Go.

c.) Move the Dragon folder to the Trash.

Step 4: Remove Dragon® Dictate caches.

a.) Choose Go to Folder from the Go menu.

b.) Enter the following text in the Go to Folder text box: ~/Library/Caches/ and click Go.

c.) Arrange files and folders in alphabetical order.

d.) Move all files that begin with "com.Dragon .dictate" to the Trash.

Step 5: Remove Dragon® Dictate preferences.

a.) Choose Go to Folder from the Go menu.

b.) Enter the following text in the Go to Folder text box: ~/Library/Preferences/ and click Go.

c.) Arrange files and folders in alphabetical order.

d.) Move all files that begin with "com.Dragon dictate" to the Trash.

Step 6: Remove Dragon Dictate Saved application state p-list file.

a.) Choose Go to Folder from the Go menu.

b.) Enter the following text in the Go to Folder text box: ~/Library/Saved Application State/ and click Go.

c.) Arrange files and folders in alphabetical order.

d.) Move all files that begin with "com.Dragon .dictate" to the Trash.

Step 7: Backup user Voice Profile.

a.) Choose Documents from the Go menu.

b.) Move all files with filenames ending in ".Dragon profile" to the Trash.

Step 8 of 8: Remove Dragon® Dictate application icon on the dock.

a.) Hold down the CONTROL key then click the Dragon® Dictate application in the dock.

b.) Click Options, and then click Remove from Dock.

Cleaning Up After Your Dragon

Dictating is very convenient and can lead to huge gains in productivity. However, it can also leave behind its own set of problems. Particularly extra spaces where you don't need them. Both Dragon® Dictate and Dragon® NaturallySpeaking have a habit of leaving a leading space before you dictate something. Additionally, if you correct something in Dragon® Dictate, sometimes additional spaces can be added around the text you just corrected. It is important to edit these spaces out before you publish your manuscript. Fortunately, I have developed some easy methods to accomplish this.

First, I'll deal with the problem of leading spaces.

In Scrivener, this is best dealt with in Project Replace. To accomplish this task, you need to make sure your invisibles are on. First, copy a ¶ into your clipboard. Then click on the Project Replace button.

Paste the ¶ into the top box and press the space bar once.

Go to the bottom box and paste the ¶ again but do not press the space bar this time.

Now, press the **Replace** button. The program will give you a warning which will make you think you are about to plan the apocalypse, but it's fine — all you're doing is removing extra spaces. It's like magic! The leading spaces should be gone.

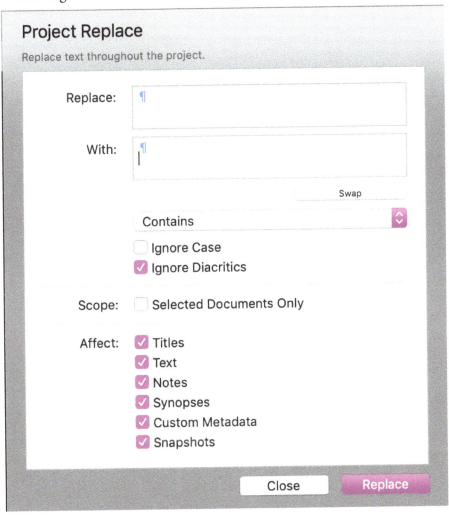

Removing Spaces before Paragraphs In Scrivener

In Microsoft Word, the process is similar, but the vernacular is different. For Word, you need to use Find and Replace. In the top box, type **^p** and then **press the space bar**. In the bottom box, type **^p**. Click **Replace All**.

All the leading spaces should now be gone.

Removing Spaces before Paragraphs in Word

The process is similar for removing double spaces. In Scrivener, go to Project Replace and **type two spaces** in the top box and **one space** in the bottom box, then click the **Replace** button.

In Microsoft Word, use the Find and Replace function to remove extra spaces. In the top box, type **two spaces** and in the bottom box, type only **one space**. Click **Replace All**. This should resolve the issue.

Chapter 10

Closing Thoughts

There's no possible way I could answer every possible question about voice recognition software in a single book. However, I hope this overview has enabled you to look at dictation in a new light and maybe encouraged you to add this tool to your workflow.

I understand dictation may not work for everyone and that's fine. But, I hope you'll read this book and give it another try if you've tried it before in the past and been frustrated.

Voice recognition software has made a profound difference in my life. Had it not been for the efforts of my vocational rehabilitation counselor, Linda James and Larry Allen, from Softnet, who provided me with software and equipment recommendations very early in my academic career, I have no idea what path my life would have taken. I don't know if dictation will make that kind of difference in any of the lives of the people who read this book, but I hope my experiences will help someone else along the way.

If you have questions, I post regularly on the Dragon® Riders board on Facebook and routinely answer questions. I can always be reached at my website MaryCrawfordAuthor.com where you will find links to my Facebook page and Twitter account as well as my email address. I hope you go forth and write productively. The world needs your words.

Resources

Retailers and Equipment:

- Nuance® (Nuance.com) — the software company which develops and supports Dragon® Dictate, Dragon® NaturallySpeaking, and Dragon® Anywhere.

- KnowBrainer (Knowbrainer.com) — a software and adaptive equipment online retailer with comprehensive resources and an active forum and helpful equipment guides.

- Blue Mic (https://www.bluedesigns.com) — The manufacturer of Yeti, Snowball, Raspberry microphones (among others). These are among the best microphones I've ever used for voice recognition software.

- TalkTech (https://talktech.com/) — This company provides a privacy mask for dictating in public. Although initially developed for court reporters, they have products available for voice recognition users too.

Internet Communities:

- Dragon Riders (https://www.facebook.com/groups/1648134245442422/) — This forum, covering both Dragon® NaturallySpeaking and Dragon® Dictate, is the most active group on Facebook. There are many participants who are well-versed in both programs and generous with their advice.

- Dragon® NaturallySpeaking Users (https://www.facebook.com/groups/Dragon® users/) — This group is also a Facebook group, but it's focus tends to be tailored toward NaturallySpeaking.

Sprinting Groups and Other Resources:

- Grotto Garden (https://www.facebook.com/groups/GrottoGarden/) — Need a sprinting partner any time, day or night? Not a problem with this friendly group of folks. Just hop on and introduce yourself. The group is large enough that there are usually sprints happening around the clock.

- Sprinting with Friends (https://www.facebook.com/groups/773369349401931/) — Is Facebook too much of a temptation? This sprinting group might be for you. The sprints actually take place in a Chatzy group. It is a great group for keeping you on task and accountable.

- NaNoWriMo (http://nanowrimo.org/) – Why not join us for National Novel Writing Month? Not only is it a fun challenge, you'll meet lots of other great writers and find a website chock full of great writing tips and prompts. It's also a great way to practice sprinting and wind discounts on software and editing programs.

- My Write Club (http://www.mywriteclub.com) — this is a great little motivating sprinting site. I love this site because it is so flexible. You can join a group sprint which is a group of random people. They have twenty-five minute sprints at the top and bottom of every hour. You can race against a group of people. You earn stars along the way for your progress which is incredibly motivating. You can also set up your own private sprint by yourself or with a group of friends. You can track your progress toward your goal.

- The Creative Penn https://www.thecreativepenn.com/tag/dictation/ — Joanna Penn has a phenomenal site with great resources for authors. She has a page dedicated to dictation.

Software and Books:

- Speech Productivity (http://www.speechproductivity.eu/) — this $25 add-in program for Dragon® Professional Individual for Windows is everything Dragon® Pad should be but isn't. I'm a huge fan.

- Literature and Latte (https://www.literatureandlatte.com/) — Scrivener is their signature program (although they do make others.) It is my go to writing program. I own three versions of it.

- Grammarly (Grammarly.com) — A web-based grammar checking program. They offer both free and paid versions. Aside from Scrivener, this is my favorite place to dictate.

- ProWritingAid (https://prowritingaid.com) — a fee-based grammar checking program. You can buy a lifetime subscription. This program is particularly good at picking up homonyms and other errors created by using voice recognition software.

- Pacemaker Press (https://www.pacemaker.press) — One of the ways I stay motivated is to track my progress. My favorite way to do this is with Pacemaker Press. I can track multiple projects and plan out my year.

- *The Writer's Guide to Training Your Dragon: Using Speech Recognition Software to Dictate Your Book and Supercharge Your Writing Workflow* by Scott Baker (https://scottbakerbooks.com/books/ — a comprehensive guide to both Dragon® NaturallySpeaking and Dragon® Dictate. He includes information on using Parallels or Boot Camp to run Dragon® NaturallySpeaking on a Mac

- *Fool Proof Dictation: A No-Nonsense System for Effective & Rewarding Dictation* by Christopher Downing (https://foolproofoutline.wordpress.com/2017/07/09/coming-soon-interested/) — a series of comprehensive exercises to build up your skills and confidence to help you become an expert at dictation.

- *Dragon Professional Individual For Dummies* by Stephanie Diamond (https://www.dummies.com/store/product/Dragon® -Professional-Individual-For-Dummies-5th-Edition.productCd-1119171032.html) — this is the single most comprehensive guide to Dragon® Professional Individual for Windows I've run across. It covers the material in much more depth, including some more information on commands and scripting.

- *The 8-Minute Writing Habit for Novelists: Triple Your Writing Speed and Learn Dictation to Produce More Words, Faster* by Monica Leonelle (https://theworldneedsyourbook.com/dictationresources) — This book incorporates dictation into an overall strategy of writing faster. Dictation is just one component of a mindset of increasing your productivity.

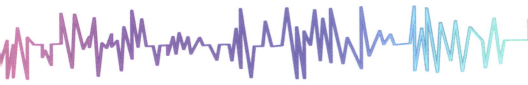

Acknowledgements

My list of acknowledgments is long and varied for this book.

Thank you to Craig Martelle, and the good folks over at 20Booksto50K® for giving me a platform to share my knowledge with other authors.

I am grateful to the input I received from Nuance® which helped me ensure that I gave accurate information.

This book would be a mess if it were not for help from Lacie Redding as my editor, Deena Rae Harrison Schoenfeldt as my formatter and an assist with my cover from Trish Ruschke Rice.

Kudos to my beta and proofreading team. Thanks Kathy, Lisa, Justin, and Wten. Your attention to detail is amazing.

Special thanks to Michelle Campbell-Scott for her work in indexing this book, so you can find order among my rambling thoughts. I appreciate your hard work.

I'd like to acknowledge great authors who have written wonderful books on this topic before me and contributed to discussions and forums on the Internet. It is through your efforts that we've brought the use of dictation to the forefront and made books like this possible. Thank you for your contributions.

As always, thanks to my family for your support and your patience as I sit in front of my computer day in and day out and speak as if I've got something important to say. Thank you for always being in my corner.

About the Author

I have been lucky enough to live my own version of a romance novel. I married the guy who kissed me at summer camp. He told me on the night we met that he was going to marry me and be the father of my children.

Eventually, I stopped giggling when he said it, and we will soon celebrate our 30th wedding anniversary. We have two children. The oldest is a Doctor of Osteopathy. He is across the United States completing his residency, but when he's done, he is going to come back to Oregon and practice Family Medicine. Our youngest son is now tackling high school. He is an author and hopes to be a mechanic when he grows up.

I write full time now. I have published over two dozen books and have several more underway. I volunteer my time to a variety of causes. I have worked as a Civil Rights Attorney and diversity advocate. I spent several years working for various social service agencies before becoming an attorney.

In my spare time, I love to cook, decorate cakes and of course, I obsessively, compulsively read.

I would be honored if you would take a few moments out of your busy day to check out my website,

MaryCrawfordAuthor.com. While you're there, you can sign up for my newsletter and get a free book. I will be announcing my upcoming books and giving sneak peeks as well as sponsoring giveaways and giving you information about other interesting events.

If you have questions or comments, please E-mail me at Mary@ MaryCrawfordAuthor.com or find me on the following social networks:

Facebook: www.facebook.com/authormarycrawford
Website: MaryCrawfordAuthor.com
Twitter: www.twitter.com/MaryCrawfordAut

Index